For Keli

Best wishes!

INSUFFERABLE INDIFFERENCE

THE MOCKING OF AMERICA

AN ADULT NONFICTION NOVEL

BY

NEIL E. CLEMENT

Copyright © 2013 Neil E. Clement.

All rights reserved. No part of this book may be reproduced, stored, or transmitted by any means—whether auditory, graphic, mechanical, or electronic—without written permission of both publisher and author, except in the case of brief excerpts used in critical articles and reviews. Unauthorized reproduction of any part of this work is illegal and is punishable by law.

Cover Content & Cover Photography
Copyright © 2013 by MTCC Publishing Company LLC,
All Rights Reserved.

Any quoted statement in this book is the intellectual property of the respective author and is reproduced herein with gratitude and with only the greatest of respect and admiration for the inestimable contribution made by each individual so quoted.

ISBN: 978-0-9895378-2-7 (sc)
ISBN: 978-0-9895378-1-0 (e)

MTCC Publishing Company LLC
www.mtccpc.com

Dedications

This book is dedicated:

to my Father: Robert Marshall Clement, retired 30-year Navy officer and the best Dad a man could have, who showed me how to more fully appreciate life in all its myriad aspects and that you only get out of it what you are willing to put into it;

and

to my Stepfather: Freeman Allen Neuschwanger, posthumously, retired Air Force and the best stepDad a kid could ask for, who taught me that hard work and perseverance can pay rich dividends;

and

to my 2nd Stepfather: Dr. Ellsworth Choate 'E.C.' Bartlett, "Doc", posthumously, ranchhand turned M.D., who taught me that life really is stranger than fiction and that a healthy skepticism must be carefully balanced with a firm belief in the obvious;

and

last but not the least bit least

to my Son: Evan Allen Clement, not retired and the best Son a man could have, who continues to convince me that staying positive when the chips are down truly is the best thing to do.

Table of Contents

Chapter 01 - What's It All About? 1

Chapter 02 - In the Beginning 16

Chapter 03 - Growing Up In Albuquerque 25

Chapter 04 - Living Overseas As A
    Teenage Military Dependent 39

Chapter 05 - Career 44

Chapter 06 - Career Turning Point 57

Chapter 07 - Disability Denied! 67

Chapter 08 - The Postscript That Became a Chapter 80

Chapter 09 - Automobile Insurance Claim Processing 89

Chapter 10 - Other Bones to Pick 100

Chapter 11 - This Phony Drug War and the Morality Police 105

Chapter 12 - Missygirl the Calico Cat 124

Chapter 13 - Officialdom Gone Crazy 126

Chapter 14 - Self-Evident Truths 137

Chapter 15 - From Here to Wherever 143

Chapter 01

WHAT'S IT ALL ABOUT?

Deep Thoughts. That's what I get when I have Time to Think. Like so:

The Process of Creation, by necessity, consists of a series of Events occurring in Some Particular Order.

Some Amount of Time is required to perform even one step of one Event.

The making of Time itself, were it possible, would be an Event.

Which points out a conundrum for the ages: It would take Time to make Time.

Real chicken and egg stuff, eh?

I figure if I can get enough of them there synapses crackling at the same time you never know what kind of Deep Thoughts might leak out of all those brain cells. Now, I can say "them there" (not to mention "I figure") and get away with it because I originally hail from the deep south, y'all, although I long ago left the area and lost my accent as well.

Deep Thinking is an activity I've had more Time to indulge in of late because a peculiar permanent disability keeps me home more often than not and there isn't much else to do. Since I am no longer being paid to spend the bulk of my time working for someone else, and therefore being distracted by having to think about their problems, I can devote all available neurons to pondering that which *I* find interesting instead. A rare privilege indeed!

Fortunately, although the word fortunately seems strangely inappropriate here, as a Theoretical Deductionist, I enjoy having Time to Think, and my current physical condition has given me just this, at least to some degree. Some dark clouds really do have a silver lining.

However, and that's a *big* however, my actual physical condition is anything but advantageous and certainly not anything I would wish anyone else to experience nor do I desire to continue in this mode any longer than I have to. I freely admit to using Deep Thinking as an escape mechanism whenever I can manage it to help take my mind off what ails me.

I won't promise not to have more Deep Thoughts as this narrative unfolds. I will pledge to keep them thought provoking. Revolutionary, even. Amusing, if at all possible, because humor is a necessary requisite for a full and rich life experience. Along with music. But enough about me. Let us think for a moment about you.

I started this book with every intention of accurately describing the circumstances surrounding this odd condition that I find myself in and to relate my experiences with both the Social Security Administration, better known as the SSA, and even better known to me as the inept autocratic federal agency that has been giving me the runaround for over five years now, and the 'No Fault Law' of Michigan, as interpreted by the automobile insurance company that is supposed to be responsible for paying all my accident related medical bills 'for life'.

Then I thought about how ridiculously boring my subject matter is and I realized that not many folks would be able to get beyond the first paragraph without falling asleep. I know it would be a tough sell for me.

Hence the Deep Thoughts, which are completely homegrown, can go in any direction and are totally unrelated to any academic degree or pedigree, since I currently have none of these with which to impress you. I offer them purely as food for thought and disavow any complicity with mainstream physics.

These Deep Thoughts come with no warranties, express or implied, as to fitness of merchantability. This does not mean the information being imparted is wrong or misleading. Oh, contraire! Controversial, maybe, but noteworthy.

There Are Things You Need To Know About Your World That I Feel Obligated to Share With You, Things That I Have Learned By Direct Experience That May Have An Impact On Your Life.

In other words, I feel the need to speak up.

My personal experiences with rank injustice on multiple occasions makes me something of an authority on the subject.

But I must perforce tell you a little something about myself first so you will know I'm not just an angry, grumpy old man yakkin' out of spite. Even though this would be easy enough to do and I have every right to feel this way, it rubs against the grain and is exactly the type of behavior I try to avoid.

My peculiar physical condition colors my every thought and prevents me from working full time. I would take an oath on it. In fact, I already have. Twice. It also defies convention.

Living inside my spine is *something* disseminating relentless dire disturbances in the form of continuous waves of *severe* pain, *shocking* electric pain, aching, burning, itching and stinging pain, collectively or individually, and that's just the spine between the shoulder blades. Key word *continuous*, as in unrelenting; constantly nibbling away at my consciousness every single moment of every day at varying levels of intensity and which if left unchecked becomes paralyzing white hot agony, and in short order, agony that pierces each and every thought with the force of a javelin striking the ground.

I can tell you now, as an expert on the subject with ten years of up close and personal experience, that pain has two components, the *feeling* and the *intensity*, and that both of these significantly mess with your ability to Think and to Move, and in varying degrees. My sensations are extreme on both counts. More about this later.

There are no medical tests available that can confirm my condition. Pain is completely subjective in nature and cannot be measured by any external device. One never becomes used to pain but one must learn to live with it or die with it. I choose life. Pain certainly lets you know you are alive if nothing else!

I don't "look" disabled. I'm not presently paralyzed physically or mentally beyond what the pain has done to my state of mind and my ability to move as per usual nor am I otherwise incapacitated by missing limbs or mental infirmity and I do offer my sincere best wishes to anyone who is afflicted in this way. My disabling condition is entirely different in nature and even as it screws with me I try to turn it to my advantage; I try to gain strength from it because the alternative is a most unattractive proposition.

For all intents and purposes, except for the distinct wrinkles on my face caused by excessive facial scrunching, I look almost as normal as anyone else, except when walking. Nevertheless, and you'll find out why in a bit, I am as fully physically disabled as anyone can be.

My financial condition when I became unable to work full time; well, let us just say I was not yet independently wealthy, forced me to have to deal with a cold, faceless U.S. government agency which has consistently refused to acknowledge my disabling condition these last five years despite overwhelming medical evidence substantiating everything that I am telling you to be true. To the greatest extent possible, anyway.

Dealing with these people and their system when one already has one's hands full dealing with issues related to one's disability is no walk in the park.

```
Are we truly cognizant of the necessary
referent principles and have we reached the
requisite language development level to
accurately describe and efficiently communicate
the concepts behind what our reality actually
is? No? Not yet? Maybe soon. Let's check
again in a hundred years.
```

I confess to having an Abiding Curiosity about Everything and Nothing, the Desire to Understand our Reality and plenty of Time to Ponder these issues. By extension I have a natural interest in the behavioral mechanisms by which our society conducts itself and in particular any institutionalized processing system which has been foisted upon us by possibly well-intentioned but definitely sorely misguided individuals wherein we the people are the product being unduly processed like so many cattle.

I have now been chewed up and spit out on three distinctly separate occasions by the inappropriate actions of individuals employed by agencies of either local, state or federal government and once by a major insurer. Four times is more than enough for one lifetime. My legendary patience with these people has exceeded its limit and by a wide margin.

It occurs to me as I am being judged for the second time by the SSA that judges are not the only people entitled to have and write opinions. I too feel free to observe, to speculate and to compose what I hope are rational conclusions in a multiverse that is not always logically organized. I also feel free to use whatever means are at my disposal to publish these deductions for general consumption by a population that is being duped into believing they have a level of security they actually do not possess.

After all, this is America, land of the free and home of the brave, where free speech is a cherished tradition, until the censors get ahold of it anyway. My opinions may not be filled with all the legal rhetoric or fancy mathematical formulas that others favor in expressing themselves but they are nonetheless as on the level as I can make them and most likely easier to read.

One brief forward if I may:

The English language can easily be manipulated to obfuscate an issue or influence opinion simply by using what I call cleverly constructed trigger phrases. It's not so much what you say as how you say it. Duh! I will try to avoid any such stylistic editorializing although I do reserve the right to do this for illustrative purposes and will tell you beforehand if I decide to use any such technique. I strive for understanding, not the other way around.

```
"By and large, language is a tool for
concealing the truth."
  - George Carlin (1937 - 2008), Comedian
```

Insufferable Indifference - The Mocking of America

This is supposed to be a factual account. While it is my intent to open your eyes to a situation you may be unaware of, and thus these words will in some fashion influence you one way or another, I promise, to the best of my ability, not to unnecessarily embellish or otherwise sway an argument using overly colorful language. Instead, I would prefer for the circumstances to speak for themselves.

So here we go.

Let's get one thing straight right off the bat: This is no sob story. Nobody likes a whiner. No one wants to be around a complainer. Most of all me.

I give to you these words not to elicit any sympathy or other closely related emotion of any such nature but only because I feel I have an obligation to tell you what treatment you can expect to receive should you become physically disabled in some fashion making you unable to work full time and therefore possibly in need of the assistance SSA disability insurance payments can provide in helping to cover living expenses.

Review the evidence and judge for yourself if Things Should Change or Remain the Same. You owe this to yourself and your family. Seriously.

```
Can there be a place where there is no time?
Wouldn't it take time to notice there is no
time?
```

Not to be bragging, but I am no slacker. I am no stumblebum. I am not now and have never been a freeloader looking for a handout. I got up at 4:30 every morning and headed off to work for a very long time. I still rise at first light although I don't go to work anymore. I was just a regular guy doing a job and raising a family, the same thing fifty million other people were doing.

I had no intention of changing or ending my activities in pursuit of this endeavor when I was Struck Down by Unfortunate Circumstances. This fact is well documented in the SSA's own database. They mail out a periodic report for each SSN reflecting gross salary for every year since work year one explaining any so-called benefits one can expect based on 'contributions' made using a formula of their own devising. Their report shows my salary and my contributions rising higher with each passing year until my professional career was abruptly terminated in 2008.

I was working in an excellent position in a decent enough company making close to six figures annual gross with a better than average benefits package and no desire to give up the job or make any drastic changes in my lifestyle that didn't involve being upwardly mobile.

You can be certain it was not my intention at the age of 50 to exchange My Rewarding Lifestyle for The Unappealing Routine of a Disabled Retiree on a Substantially Reduced Fixed Income Facing an Uncertain Future Outlook with Major Medical Issues and No Health Insurance.

No, no, that was not My Master Plan for Retirement at all, not even close.

SSA disability payments are of a subsistence nature only and not at all a desirable retirement package, at least from my viewpoint, since they don't even begin to cover the bills I have to pay each month, which remain substantial. Not to mention the troubles being disabled can cause.

But these benefits, when combined with private insurance, can make all the difference in the world between making it and being insolvent. The inability to collect these benefits can be devastating if you have nothing else to fall back on should you become disabled and can no longer work full time.

I always had faith that should this happen to me that it would be no problem collecting the promised SSA disability insurance benefit payments. It seems to me that helping those who cannot work due to unexpected disability was the original intent of the creators of this insurance, the whole enchilada if you will, the reason behind all this stuff in the first place.

I always felt certain this financial aid would be there if needed so my family and I would not have to suffer any unnecessary economic hardship if I became unable to work full time due to accident or injury. After all, the cost for this coverage was taken out of each paycheck in the usual compulsory fashion.

Boy, was I wrong.

Were it not for the employee group long-term disability insurance policy I was covered by while working and this insurance company's willingness to pay what the SSA has refused to pay these last five years, my life and that of my extended family would have been dramatically different indeed. The fly in the ointment is that I do not know how long I can expect to receive this extra support should the SSA continue to refuse to recognize my disability although I know for sure it will stop when I turn 65, which actually isn't all that far away now.

But what really bites my goat is how I was forced to pay the premiums all those years for a compulsory insurance policy which benefits I can only collect on if some stranger agrees to this based solely on their own interpretation of my situation irrespective of my actual circumstances.

In other words, one collects SSA disability insurance benefit payments based solely on how some person feels about this and this person is not your doctor. One person, with full license to make arbitrary decisions without accountability, will decide for you if disability benefits are anything they feel you are entitled to collect. Something is not right in Kansas, folks, and the other 49 states, Puerto Rico and all the other territories are not doing all that much better.

```
If space and time were created, which one
was created first?  Don't you need the one to
make the other?
```

Under the current system of disability jurisprudence, assuming there even needs to be such a thing, it is an administrative law judge who rules on your qualification to receive any SSA disability insurance benefit payments, not your doctor, nor even any team of doctors.

One supremely unqualified individual will decide whether you may or may not collect any benefits, in their own sweet time and using their own criteria. Period. Nothing personal.

Repeat:

A complete stranger, likely with no medical training and wearing a black robe, who was appointed, not elected, who doesn't really care all that much about you or your problems, will decide in the course of a fifteen to thirty minute interview your suitability to collect the disability benefits that were supposedly guaranteed by the full faith and power of the United States government by the simplified method of taking compulsory deductions from each paycheck to cover the cost.

This Decision generally happens only after you have been kept waiting an inordinately long period of time. My own 'case' has been dragging on for more than five years now.

To add insult to injury, my personal opinion and the professional opinions of all my doctors regarding my disabling condition have been completely discounted as irrelevant for this whole time by the SSA.

Attendance at a hearing in a courtroom is mandatory. Even if you are a complete veg someone must attend the hearing as your representative. Which begs the question, if you are a complete veg, exactly why is a hearing to ascertain your disability status necessary? And let me sincerely apologize here and now to anyone who has been offended by this term but there really is no other way to put it.

Moving the venue from the medical arena to a courtroom clearly shows the intent: by definition we are all being treated as criminals.

This may be The Way It Has Always Been Done but this does not make it right. This does not make it The Way Things Should Be Done. No government agency has the right to put me on trial with no jury for a crime I have not committed simply because I have become disabled.

Making matters worse, there are apparently so many disability applications being filed and so few civil servants tending them that it can take years for your data to cross the desk of the ruling judge and this under the best of circumstances. Additionally, recent statistics show a large spike in these claims occurs whenever a recession hits the economy. I do not know if there was a corresponding hike in hiring by the SSA to handle this workload but somehow I doubt it.

Administering these funds in this fashion is tantamount to malfeasance in office and completely defeats the original purpose of this insurance. Such an administrative policy does more to alienate the population of this country than it does in assisting them. This may explain why armed guards with metal detectors are posted at

SSA offices. We are paying to protect them from us. Cute. And completely unnecessary.

```
If the Big Bang created everything then
clearly there is some way to create matter.
```

In the real world we prosecute fraud after the fact.

The established police / judiciary system serves to identify, locate, apprehend and prosecute offenders, at least some of the time. It's not perfect but it's all we got. For now. Could use improvements, I'm sure. Aside from the ludicrous 'sting' operations carried out by over-zealous fringe groups in a futile effort to police our morals or our habits, the bulk of the attention goes toward those who have allegedly committed an actual crime, and rightly so.

At least, that is the way it is supposed to work.

The fact that this system is in some ways also out of kilter vis-à-vis the interpretation of what constitutes an actual crime is a subject we will cover in more detail a bit later. For now it is enough to recognize that this system still generally puts the horse before the cart.

In the artificial SSA world everything seems to be backwards.

One is presumed fraudulent up front. One must get an attorney to represent oneself in a courtroom setting and the both of you must explain to a very skeptical lay person why one should receive the disability benefits one is claiming. Unfortunately, attorneys do not come cheap.

The medical records and the deposition(s) given by your doctor(s) are apparently not enough to prove your case. You must personally convince some person that you are not faking. Which process would certainly seem to reward good actors anyway?

Insufferable Indifference - The Mocking of America

The person judging you generally has no real expertise for correctly evaluating your specific condition. This alone should be enough to put a halt to these nefarious activities. This behavior by the rank and file members of this organization reminds me too much of the reported activities practiced by members of the Inquisition.

You will almost certainly be ordered to submit to an unnecessary and potentially humiliating physical examination by another complete stranger, and again, this person generally has no real expertise as to your specific condition. How on earth can the opinion of some random doctor, developed after a brief exam, have any amount of credibility against the weight of years of medical records and the teams of doctors responsible for recording them as you are treated for your disorder?

Now, this may sit well with some of you but it just bites me right in the craw.

I am as skeptical as the next guy, but there *are* limits. If one already has one or more doctors certifying disabled status, just why is it that one must needs also be 'judged' in the trumped up court of some self-serving civil servant? Just exactly why is it that one's medical condition need come to the attention of an alleged judge at all?

And why exactly is it necessary for this person to demand an accounting in person and then take it upon themselves as totally unqualified individuals to pass judgment as to the viability of the arguments made by said claimant under duress when the health system has already conclusively done this very thing in a somewhat less stressful setting using established medical procedures?

```
    Excerpt from Missygirl the Calico Cat Book
of Daily Quotes:
    To see or not to see, that is the key, to
your ability, to be what you want to be.
```

The people populating this contrived world we call the SSA would have us believe that the long delay experienced in processing disability claims is due to the influx of such an epidemic of false claims being filed as to completely overwhelm the resources of this woefully understaffed agency.

They would further have us believe that the system they have devised to stem the flood and weed out all the fakers up front is good and necessary but sorely overloaded and in need of bolstering and that to this end they are but humble servants toiling endlessly with the extensive backlog in an effort to eventually aid the people who are actually deserving assistance. No matter how long it takes.

The American people deserve better than this farce. What seems to completely escape the notice of these so-called experts is that they themselves are the root of the problem with their foolhardy review process.

A polite free society embraces a reasonable expectation of equality of treatment in a timely fashion. Making it difficult for any disabled individual to collect SSA disability benefit payments allegedly guaranteed by a compulsory insurance policy by artificially creating process restrictions is cruel in the extreme. Life is already difficult enough for such individuals. Such people need less roadblocks, not more.

Putting up one artificial wall after another and improperly delaying any kind of financial assistance in response to a request for help is not the correct way to conduct this business. This behavior may even violate the Americans with Disabilities Act of 1990 and if not perhaps it should. To be unjustly persecuted when you are most vulnerable due to some medical malady makes 'being processed like a side of beef' doubly horrific in nature.

By association, without disability benefit approval, there can be

Insufferable Indifference - The Mocking of America

no Medicare coverage, potentially creating a Double Whammy for the Unfortunate Recipient, who may not have the means to finance private health insurance and must instead face the brunt of paying full price out of pocket should anything actually happen requiring medical assistance.

Routine medical and dental procedures, for those who haven't checked lately, are actually quite expensive. This is assuming you want to keep your current providers. The cost of non-routine medical procedures is so high it defies belief.

Just one brief example: my most recent tooth encounter involving a root canal gone bad set me back over 1,400 smackeroos. I believe this one tooth is now worth over 3,500 shekels in the local currency. The ability to still chew my food? Priceless. It still bites though to have to pay for this service in full i.e. out-of-pocket when most everyone else has the assistance of dental insurance through their employer group policies to help cover these (really high) fees.

We should be helping people with disabilities first and going after crooks second. Period.

The folks conducting these SSA operations are delivering 'administrative justice', which by definition, should not exist. They should be engaged in administering benefits, not justice. True Justice can only be found in a real court, duly elected and empowered by the people, not in the phony 'Final Decisions' being dispensed by Those Who Think They Know Better Than You, Your Team of Doctors and the Body of Medical Evidence which gets recorded as you are treated.

But I get ahead of myself.

Chapter 02

IN THE BEGINNING

How do you know you can trust me to give you the unvarnished truth? Well, you don't. But maybe I can convince you despite yourself. This is my life we are talking about.

What makes me an authority on this subject? Well, I've had ten years to reflect on it.

How did I get where I am at today? I will tell you now.

Like many of you I lived my youth during the years of the cold war.

Born on Thanksgiving Day in '53 at a naval base hospital in northeast Florida, fifth child of alternating boys and girls brought forth over a six year span, my first few thankfully impossible to remember years were spent on the southeast coast of the good old US of A.

```
"When I was born I was so ugly the doctor
slapped my mother."
— Rodney Dangerfield (1921 - 2004), Actor,
Comedian
```

I must have been about three when the family moved to Naples,

Italy so we could be closer to Dad while he served his tour of duty. I have a permanent memento from this time in the form of a large scar on my left thumb where a Navy surgeon reattached it after I nearly sliced it clean off during an unfortunate encounter with a jar of peanut butter.

I got the story straight from sister Jean whom we fondly call The Bean. She vividly recalls the aftermath of this bloody event. Apparently I was around 4 when it happened.

I have a flicker of a memory standing in the kitchen of our Naples apartment with our nanny bustling about somewhere nearby and seeing a jar of peanut butter sitting on the counter. I will assume that as the always hungry type I just naturally had to have some. If I concentrate hard enough I can get a flash memory of picking up the jar, then trying to catch it as it slipped out of tiny hands.

I still cannot remember what happened after this although, as I said, my sister filled in a lot of the details. Apparently my hands caught up to the jar just as it struck the tile floor, an Event precipitating unfavorable results for the both of us. My mind may have suppressed any memory of the actual moment when exploding glass shards met unprotected thumb but I am quite sure it must have been profoundly painful and shocking in the extreme.

I was trundled off to the navy hospital toot sweet with my wounded hand and its dangling thumb wrapped in a sheet. So skillfully was this digit reattached that it grew and performed as if nothing had happened to it although if I accidentally bang it on something it hurts like the devil! Even now.

The theorized Big Bang did *not* create a causality wherein Nothing became Everything. *Everything* did *not* bang *into* Nothing from

Nothing. The very notion of such a thing is preposterous.

We don't really know what, if anything, was banged into or where/what/when it banged from even if we do call it a singularity. But *it* wasn't Nothing.

Something became *Something Else*.

We banged into 'our' Space, empty or otherwise, from *Somewhere Else* using *Somewhat Else* during *Somewhen Else*.

Probably not for the first time and probably not for the last.

Of course, this is only one opinion amongst many.

I have to believe that I became well acquainted with old man pain early on as a result of this experience even if I can't remember it now. 'Normal' pain, the kind that eventually fades away.

My first really strong memories come from living on Kirtland Air Force Base in Albuquerque, New Mexico. We moved there in '58 because this selfsame sister had asthma really bad and her doctor convinced my parents that the high, dry air would provide substantial relief for her. And he was right.

At school we were instructed on how to 'duck and cover' if any intercontinental ballistic missiles carrying multiple nuclear warheads just happened to be launched our way by the Soviet Union. There was a film clip the teacher played for the class using one of those loud old flickering projectors and rolls of extremely flammable celluloid tape which threw picture images on a screen if you had one, or on the wall if you didn't, showing just how to do this.

Insufferable Indifference - The Mocking of America

We practiced ducking and covering using our school desks for extra cover. Over time we learned that in the event of an actual emergency if we ducked far enough we could more effectively kiss our asses' goodbye.

It is difficult to visualize our entire universe expanding to its present size from an almost infinitesimally small, almost infinitely dense point, and even more difficult to believe it happened so fast it took practically no Time at all. This Theory of Inflation is curious at best.

It is even more difficult to visualize our entire universe seething at a temperature so high it ceases to be a temperature at all as much as a condition or a state.

Yet physicists have found evidence suggesting this may have been what our reality was like in the Far Distant Past.

This inflation theory goes something like this:

Something, Almost Infinitely Dense and exceedingly tiny, smaller than an atom, performed an incredibly fast exponential spatial expansion, either already being or becoming Almost Infinitely Hot in the process, and in so doing 'created' what we now view as our universe.

This (inflated) volume of space then began cooling. Eventually Subatomic Particles appeared (or were formed) followed by the first stars.

This sounds suspiciously like an unbelievably enormous, virtually unlimited energy transfer and leaves us with several basic questions. What heated up to such fantastic mind-boggling temperatures and why? Why did it cool off?

Where did all the heat go?

I was an average student if memory serves. Got by with C's mostly. Sometimes worse, sometimes better. Which is what average means, right?

I guess you could say my family was middling middle class although I know now that Mother struggled more than once to make ends meet but never let on that anything was amiss. As if I would have noticed!

We never went hungry that I can recall even if we did sometimes have lots of macaroni and cheese for dinner. Kidding, just kidding! This *was* a popular food item though and we did have it frequently. Homemade, of course; the only kind worth eating.

As the last child I was given many hand-me-downs to wear and was glad to have them. Most of the time anyway. Not kidding!

We were indoctrinated by the Propaganda Mill of the day to believe in and to try to achieve The American Dream: a secure job; a house of your own with a well-appointed garage and two cars in the driveway; a chicken on the dinner table any night you wanted, not just on Sunday, etc. etc. If one worked hard enough one could have one's own share of the pie! Cherry pie even! That was the mantra.

You could see the evidence all over the country as education, industry and construction on the one hand and arts and entertainment on the other all exploded with new activity on many different fronts.

Spearheading this effort: Intense Scientific Research at major universities. The Potential Profits that can be realized from all the new discoveries that were being made encouraged the creation of many new private companies bringing about a host of New Inventions and Innovations in many recognized disciplines and especially chemistry and engineering.

Modern Life was now possible for virtually everyone. The need to produce sufficient quantities of goods for such a large population spurred big improvements in manufacturing techniques for the long established assembly line process.

Amazing new products were introduced by the infant information storage and retrieval technology companies as they pushed the limits of the miniaturization of electronic components.

The research and development being done by the burgeoning pharmaceutical and medical supply companies continued lengthening human lifespan while at the same time improving the quality of life.

Banking, insurance and investment firms were taking full advantage of the information systems revolution and leapfrogging one another to get a piece of the action to become the juggernauts we have today.

Advertising began really taking off as a major force even without the use of the much discussed subliminal effect, as well as the fashion industry.

The entertainment and hospitality industries were developing new products and strategies and growing as fast as they could put up new parks and complexes. We can in large part thank Mr. Walt Disney for this latter activity.

The intellectual revolution that began at the end of the Dark Ages was finally beginning to bear fruit. Everyone could now live better than royalty. Anyone could become a billionaire. This was an unprecedented event in human history.

```
We can conjecture that Time had no beginning
and will have no end but this would be idle
speculation because there is no way to prove
it. Still, it seems to be the only explanation
that makes any sense.
```

New Mexico is a great place to live. There is a good bit of desert land but there is much more than this. Heavily forested mountains raise their peaks high above the dry dusty mesas on which they sit providing ample ski destinations in winter. In the summertime you can find expansive high meadows filled to the brim with tall, thickly growing grass and many varieties of wildflowers blooming everywhere you look.

The largest reservoir in the state, Elephant Butte Lake, where I spent many enjoyable summer weekends, sits on the Rio Grande south of Socorro with I25 running alongside of it and offers many summertime activities unavailable elsewhere in the state except at a few other relatively large reservoirs such as the always too cold Bluewater Lake in the west and Conchas Lake in the east.

Photographers love this place and with good reason. Lush valleys and high mountain ranges have surprisingly frequent creeks and rivers fed by rain or snow pack and the abundant wide open spaces offer many magnificent and dramatic vistas. The landscape generally ranges from sandy brown to burnt sienna although vibrant colors abound and are easily visible when traveling through the state.

Many hillsides and outcrops are yellow to orange to red in color and provide spectacular splashes of color. All shades of green but mostly sage and scrub oak can be seen scattered about as low-to-the-ground desert growth infiltrates every possible niche. The endless blue sky provides a stunning backdrop for this picturesque landscape. Clouds seem to climb all the way to the edge of space.

Some wildlife can still be found surviving in the more remote regions despite the onslaught of man. All of this can be found along with enough white sand to make as many new beaches as you want.

New Mexico truly is an enchanting place just as the state motto says.

Evidence has been uncovered proving that people, as in hominids, have been in the Americas for at least 50,000+ years, quite likely far longer. The Clovis culture, so named because of artifacts found near the town of Clovis in the early 20th century, maintained active habitations in the region as recently as 10,000 and as much as 13,000 years ago. These people are thought to have been the genesis for all native American cultures arising since.

```
Available evidence indicates that energetic
radiation of some kind initially populated our
reality with, well, reality.  Maybe more than
one kind of radiation.
    This radiation came from somewhere, it wasn't
just spontaneously manufactured by magic.
    Our universe may be the result of nothing
more than some kind of vast recycling process
in action.
    The real question is: where did All Creation
come from in the first place?  And the ultimate
real question is: was there a first place?
```

Albuquerque is an oasis in the desert situated next to some rather large mountain peaks; the Sandia and Manzano ranges come together here, part of the Rocky Mountain chain. Quite nice mountains actually and nicely forested. The desert can be quite nice too as long as you have enough water, which, thanks to a massive underground aquifer in the area, we did.

The Rio Grande flows through the valley from the north on its way to the Gulf of Mexico when it flows at all. The land here lies mostly flat proceeding in a long gently sloping grade from the river east about twenty miles to the Sandia Mountains and west about fifteen miles to the high mesa and eventually more mountains.

You can see Mount Taylor in the distance to the west, where, rumor has it, many magic mushrooms have been found. This landscape is picture perfect for building a large city and shazam! if this isn't exactly what happened.

Chapter 03

Growing Up In Albuquerque

Albuquerque proper was a much smaller place in the late fifties because it wasn't all that built up like it is now. Much of the land in the valley was undeveloped or used only for farming. The west mesa and the eastside heights were almost completely vacant, just empty land with desert brush, crabgrass and tumbleweeds.

An incredible 60-year building boom has changed all that. Vacant land is now at a premium. The view of the city at night from on high is truly spectacular!

If you want to see what the land looked like back then you can view old photographs or you can go and look at the native American tribal land in the area to the north of Tramway Road between I25 and the mountain slopes.

Not very many naval forces were stationed in this place due to the lack of any large body of water in the area, including my Dad, who spent most of his time working on an aircraft carrier which, needless to say, came no closer than the nearest coastal naval base in California or Florida.

Dad did come and visit as often as possible between assignments and these occasions were habitually festive and not just because he always came bearing gifts: useful stuff like wrist watches and clothing. We would always go out to eat at a very popular local cafeteria whose name sounded like a mink's coat. Good food!

Growing up in this *other* mile-high city during this extraordinary era was interesting to say the least.

Christmas in this region, albeit quite a young tradition, was particularly enchanting, a really magical time, perhaps because of all the palpable ancient footsteps in the area, or perhaps because the unbelievably huge luminaria displays in the neighborhoods surrounding the zoo were so lavish and spectacular as to defy the imagination. The *feeling* was tangible enough. Strange but true. Perhaps it was the earth's own magnetic field doing weird stuff. Who knows? Perhaps it was because I was a Kid at Christmastime just feeling the Anticipation of The Day.

Albuquerque was growing by leaps and bounds, thanks in part to the presence of the huge Sandia military base and its research laboratories, the University of New Mexico campus, the statewide agriculture and livestock explosion and the largest airport in the area still known as the Sunport servicing Santa Fe, Taos and Los Alamos National Laboratories, the place where the first atom bomb was developed, remember that?

Experiencing childhood in Albuquerque during the late fifties and sixties and witnessing all the incredible changes occurring nationwide during this time was, at the risk of sounding cliché, truly a once in a lifetime event. Truly an idyllic period. Except for the constant threat of annihilation.

If the space in the universe has always been expanding from the smaller-than-an-atom point that was its genesis, what exactly was there before this; in other words, what is it our space is replacing as it expands; what is on the other side of the edge of the universe?

It doesn't hurt Albuquerque any to have Old Town at the intersection of Central Avenue (Route 66) and Rio Grande Boulevard, where many native artisans still peddle authentic Indian artifacts: jewelry, pottery, rugs, blankets, leather; you know, stuff like that. Much of it very good stuff.

If you tire of this commercial scene you can go across the highway and visit the Albuquerque Zoo and associated Nature Park which is not far away just to the south along the Rio Grande on the other side of the Country Club. Great place to walk! Once you drive there. It would be quite a hike from Old Town.

Highway construction and maintenance was ongoing everywhere in the country to handle the huge numbers of new cars that were being put on the road, but more importantly for the phalanx of trucks the booming post war economy was churning out to transport all the new furniture, appliances and other consumer goods that were being produced by all the new factories.

Freedom was as close as your driveway! You could go anywhere in the country whenever you wanted to assuming you could afford to do so. All you had to do was pack a bag and hop in the car. Gasoline was what, 15 to 20 cents a gallon?

The vast majority of these highways were two lane roads that passed through thriving small towns all along the way. Which meant you had to periodically slow down or get slapped with a speeding ticket. Sometimes you got slapped anyway.

If you didn't want to drive you could always invoke the bus, train or plane option.

My family, now with step-father Freeman driving, made the trip from Albuquerque to South Carolina on multiple occasions. Good ole' two-lane Route 66. We took that road almost all the way across the country. And back. Repeatedly. All seven of us in one car. For days on end. My place was usually in the back of the station wagon, the fold down seat all the way in the back facing the rear window.

The ride was mostly pure boredom since there wasn't much to do but sit there looking out the window. We did give many a truck driver the old arm pump to encourage horn blowing. It worked more often than not. A great bunch of people, our truck drivers. I have always admired them. Their job is not an easy one.

I'm pretty sure we made Oklahoma City the first night and Little Rock the next, then on to Knoxville and finally Spartanburg, South Carolina, the area where both sets of my grandparents lived. I can still remember when crossing the Mississippi near Memphis was a big deal. At least it was for a seven-going-on-eight year old boy whose experience with any big river was confined to the normally bone-dry Rio Grande.

We slept in a variety of hotels, pool mandatory, and ate in nearby restaurants with an emphasis on home cooking. Waffles were a big favorite! For a young kid it was pretty exciting to have so many new things to see and places to explore. So many interesting things along the way!

The billboards situated all along the roadway promised surprise and adventure for only a small fee! Huge underground caverns! Big snakes! The best fudge anywhere! Home cooking! There were many fireworks outlets, all of which we bypassed because those found at our destination were always cheaper.

The Great Plains took *forever* to cross but eventually the Great

Smokey Mountains came into view. Crossing through these was always visually stimulating because of all the sudden elevation changes and the breathtaking mountain scenery which came as a refreshing change from the monotonous flat countryside to the west. Care had to be taken to move slowly on the switchbacks or for sure someone would get sick. Maybe more than one someone.

```
Time clearly has its moments.
You can't see them.  But you can feel them.
We do not actually measure Time, we measure duration; we measure the elapsed 'Time' between moments.  I believe we are still trying to figure out what a moment really is.
```

Once back in Albuquerque we spent most of our time outside riding our bikes or playing games. The weather was generally very accommodating. We had moderate temperatures and clear skies with scattered clouds virtually every day.

Some of the games we played in no particular order:

Hide and Seek: "Olly Olly Oxen Free!"

Chase: "Tag, You're It!"

Marbles, jacks and pickup sticks. I wish I still had some of those marbles today.

Horseshoes: Far more difficult than it appears.

Cowboys and Indians: We built forts out of any available material, cardboard boxes being a particular favorite; sticks, dirt and rocks the only alternative when no cardboard was available, or even just a line in the sand, although we would occasionally pile tumbleweeds; then we proceeded to try to extinguish one another.

Cops and Robbers: "bang you're dead". This game, along with

the previous one, typically didn't last very long. Hard to play when you're supposed to be dead.

We would jump around on Pogo sticks when we had them but they didn't really work all that well back then. One grows weary fairly quickly of bouncing up and down even when they did work so this game didn't last long either.

That kind of thing.

Inside we had board games like Scrabble and card games like '52 Pickup' which I can reliably report is a very short game indeed.

Tic Tac Toe was a favorite because you could play it just about anywhere. Darts. And of course 'Rock, Paper, Scissors' for making important decisions.

Entertainment-wise we had nothing electronic except radio and television.

There was one telephone line with maybe two extensions, usually a wall phone in the kitchen and a table phone in the living room, the kind you can only find in antique stores now. A transistor radio was a real novelty!

The TV in the living room was a small wooden box with one convex glass side displaying really sharp, crisp, realistic black and white moving picture images of really small people proportionally matched to their surroundings. And it spoke! Just like magic! Or radio.

The TV stations actually closed up shop and went off the air each night! All four channels! But only after playing the *Star Spangled Banner* with a U.S. flag waving back and forth in the breeze; sometimes real and sometimes animated.

Morning, noon and night would be nonstop soap operas, prize shows, variety shows, comedy shows, drama and mystery, sports, westerns and news reports. These subjects dominated the

Insufferable Indifference - The Mocking of America

programming on each station. There were occasional interruptions for commercial advertising, because TV was free! but the station had to make money somehow or go out of business, and, best of all, cartoons!

There were not very many cop shows that I can remember although Dragnet was busy establishing this brand and proved to be quite popular. In black and white of course.

Color TV made quite a splash when it came out! Oh my, yes! It looked really goofy at first. The colors were not always quite right.

The airwaves were rife with imaginary hero tales every evening while Saturday morning was filled with animated fables. The advertising industry took off like a rocket to help other businesses and themselves cash in on the popularity of this constant entertainment stream.

You will forgive me I trust but I must list some of these unforgettable characters:

That amazing white horse Silver and his good friend The Lone Ranger (mustn't forget Tonto); Superman (*golly* Mr. Kent!); Audie Murphy (a *real* hero); Roy Rogers and Dale Evans (singing sensations); Rin Tin Tin the wonder dog (worth reading about); Lassie the other wonder dog (and Timmy); there was only one Rin Tin Tin but there were many Lassies; Buck Rogers with really goofy graphics; Flash Gordon vs. Ming the Merciless, also with really goofy graphics; Zorro! Ai caramba!, excellent sword play, exciting adventures and (yuck) romance; the list of real and imaginary heroes goes on and on and constituted what passed for role models for proper civilized, and in some cases uncivilized, behavior. They left quite an impression.

```
    The existence of space and time means there
   must  be   antispace   somewhere   and   antitime
```

somewhen.

It was somehow hilarious to watch some cartoon character get smashed as flat as a pancake knowing full well that in the next instant he (yes, he, never she) would spring back to normal size, completely unhurt, or for more laughs, get stretched into some other unnatural configuration!

Cartoon characters were routinely hacked to pieces or blown to bits. No permanent damage was ever done that I can remember. To them or to me. It was pure make-believe nonstop entertainment, period.

Forgive me again if you will for listing some of them here but I feel they are noteworthy. Feel free to skip the next paragraph.

Bugs Bunny (another real hero! with all due respect to the inestimable Mr. Murphy!); Mighty Mouse ("*here* today to save the *day*"); Daffy Duck, Porky Pig and Elmer Fudd, doesn't get much wackier than these three; Foghorn J. Leghorn ("*Boy*, I say, *boy* you can't *do* that") and his friends The Dog and Henery the 'Chicken' Hawk; Heckle and Jeckle the wisecracking crows; Mickey Mouse, Donald Duck and company; Yosemite Sam; poor Wile E. Coyote and the rascally Roadrunner; the Tasmanian Devil; Tweety Bird and his 'putty tat' Sylvester who, when not being outfoxed by the innocent feathered yellow fellow, was constantly being outwitted by Speedy Gonzalez, the fastest mouse anywhere; poor Tom & that mischievous mouse Jerry; and who could forget Chip N' Dale, those ever so polite chipmunks?; Felix the Cat (whoa!); in the early sixties we got Yogi Bear and his constant companion Boo Boo. What a riot!

My apologies to any I have left out and kudos to those who contributed this comedic dimension to American culture. Special thanks go to Mel Blanc and son!

Insufferable Indifference - The Mocking of America

"Just when I discovered the meaning of life, they changed it."
— George Carlin (1937 - 2008), Comedian

Saturday morning cartoons were the prize bestowed for doing a good job during the week. They had their own humorous message to convey and I missed very few! I didn't watch Captain Kangaroo (much) or Howdy Doody (at all) but I understand they were very popular.

Weeknights we had the unstoppable Marshall Dillon on Gunsmoke and the undefeatable Perry Mason (poor Hamilton Burger) along with hundreds and hundreds of other shows over the years. Lucy and Desi! The Honeymooners! Jack Benny! So funny. Combat! Not funny. The Twilight Zone! Thank you: Rod Serling. Star Trek! (1966) Thank you: Gene Roddenberry. I lived for Saturday night and the next installment! Speaking of Saturday night, I must give honorable mention to SNL (1975) as not only one of the longest running shows in the U.S., but is in my opinion the best comedy / variety / entertainment show of all time. Thank you: Lorne Michaels.

The concept that good always triumphs over evil was replayed over and over and over in so many variations it made you want to believe it was actually true.

And the movies! Don't get me started.

The music!! So much good music! From Mozart to modern day rock and roll. Fabulous! One genius after another. Blues guitar players! One genius after another, but not so many we could afford to lose a single one.

So much stuff to read!

In addition to all the classics we had Zane Grey and Louis L'Amour for thrilling western themed stories. Robert E. Howard wrote the best action fantasy bar none! No greater hero than the mighty Conan ever walked the earth.

Robert A. Heinlein wrote fantastic science fiction aimed specifically at young boys before going on to do other very amazing stuff clearly oriented more towards adult readers. I believe *Stranger in a Strange Land* (1961) was the first of these somewhat racy stories he would not have been able to publish sooner because of the governmental and / or publisher censorship practices being forced on the industry (and society) at the time.

Isaac Asimov, Ray Bradbury, Edgar Rice Burroughs, Arthur C. Clarke, Frederik Pohl, A.E. Van Vogt and a score of other authors contributed a rich background tapestry of thoughts and ideas, and before them all H. G. Wells and Jules Verne. Thank you Hugo Gernsback and John W. Campbell!

The Hardy Brothers and Nancy Drew offered engrossing mystery adventures for young readers. Life was good! Even school was OK because of all the neat stuff I was learning there.

```
The theory of Inflation says we didn't really
Bang at all.  It was apparently more of a
whoosh.

A whoosh that happened so fast the speed of
light is reduced to the pace of the slowest
snail that ever lived.  Times a few billion.
The theory says: One nano-nano-nano-nanosecond
there was no Space (or Time or anything else)
and in the next nano-nano-nano-nanosecond there
was.
```

"OK, so what's the speed of dark?"

Insufferable Indifference - The Mocking of America

— Steven Wright (1955 -), Comedian

The expanse of Space we see today materialized so fast you might as well say it happened all at once even if we do assign some fraction of a second as to the actual duration necessary for the expansion to complete.

Since we are using Time to measure how long it took for Inflation to occur, it would seem obvious that Time was already available to permit said measurement. So much for the (or Time) part above. Still working on the Space part.

Recent WMAP data indicates this inflationary episode happened some 13.798 +- 0.037 billion years ago. This figure is based on how long the light has been traveling toward us from the oldest thing we can see, the Cosmic Microwave Background (CMB).

We cannot see the light from the very first stars and we never will. These objects are so far away that the light they produced hasn't had enough travel time to reach us. Moreover, this light will never shine on us because the Space between us is expanding faster than the light can travel. *Interesting.* We also cannot 'see' anything beyond the all-encompassing veil of the CMB, the Cosmic Microwave Background; it is the oldest thing we can detect with our current technology, the 'light' that has been travelling for the longest time.

Once the initial Inflation event had finished inflating the universe, every single bit of what we call the observable universe was in some kind of extremely energetic radiation / energetic (hot) state which then began cooling off.

There was no matter as we define it, only energy.

The rest, as they say, is history. That is the Theory of Inflation.

I favor the Theory of Polarization:

A switch is flipped and in that instant an entire pre-existing volume of space we now call our universe gets polarized from one state to another and perhaps back again. As if a cosmic light bulb the size of our universe came on, then immediately went off as the filament burned out from some overload condition, leaving a doozy of an afterglow!

We could blame it on the interaction or intersection of opposing forces of some kind.

Everything in our universe seems to be moving; perhaps the universe itself is moving as well and came in contact with its polar opposite precipitating a colossal universe / anti-universe hookup producing instant annihilation everywhere all at once based not on what occupied space but on space itself, whatever that is.

Any evidence of or for The Previous State

is, at the moment, beyond the veil of the CMB and was vaporized in more ways than one in any event. A complete wipe if you will.

This line of reasoning leads to one undeniable conclusion: there is no reason not to believe it couldn't happen again at any moment. Not to worry though. If such a thing does happen again we won't know it. It will happen so fast we won't have time to notice.

The extreme heat-like effect generated by this instantaneous transformation, actually a state transition, was so severe it caused Space to begin expanding in every direction, like so much warm cosmic taffy.

A whole universe seething at such an unthinkable temperature would certainly have some impact on the surrounding extra-universal Space as well, probably pushing away whatever is there, perhaps the very thing that caused the polarization to occur in the first place.

Some of the heat radiated away, meaning there must have been and still is some place for it to radiate into, more space outside our universe if you will.

This polarization effect was almost certainly limited to a finite amount of Space. Even Infinity has to break things up into manageable chunks.

In our case about 14 billion light years' worth of Space now grown to 93 billion light years in diameter. As universes go we don't really know how this stacks up size wise. We *can* say that, in comparison to Infinity, we are pretty small potatoes.

After this clean wipe, the data, the energy, began organizing, or clumping, thanks to Gravity, Time and other still Unknown Dimensional Forces. The temperature eventually subsided enough to permit some of the energy to coalesce into matter. And back again. Order out of chaos out of order, these are the results we see today.

Time passed.

Chapter 04

LIVING OVERSEAS AS A TEENAGE MILITARY DEPENDENT

Returning to Italy in '67 along with sisters Jean and Mary, by special invitation from Dad, I spent most of two very formative years attending Forrest Sherman High School, the 'American' school, then on via Manzoni overlooking Naples harbor.

We eventually found our permanent apartment on this same road situated on the fifth floor of a decent high rise building, one amongst many to be found close to the school.

What a view! Great times! What a marvelous place to be a teenager! Go Wildcats!

Here I experienced some of the best times of my life.

Living in Naples as a teenage dependent during the late sixties was just fabulous. One had the Italian culture to deal with and this was always interesting, particularly since I didn't speak the language all that well despite having been fluent as a young child. Good thing we have hands!

Most of the Italians I met were very friendly. Especially toward my sisters.

We had access to some American stuff on base at the PX which made the transition in lifestyles a bit easier.

Our first (temporary) apartment sat right next to a local rail line just outside the AFSOUTH gate. Each morning around 3 a.m. a train would go roaring past causing the entire building to quake and vibrate. This was not what you would call a quiet event. The first night was some surprise, I can tell you. The strange thing is, after a few nights of this, it became hardly noticeable.

We couldn't eat any of the fresh fruits or vegetables unless we soaked them in water with a bit of bleach first to eliminate the Hepatitis element. You might think this would change the taste but not at all. The fruits and vegetables in this region are some of the best on the planet. They are so full of flavor, thanks to the quality of the volcanic soil, that you can readily taste the difference when compared to the bland stuff on the shelves here in The World.

American citizens could always go to the USO in downtown Naples and shoot pool for free. Even though I never became the pool shark I had hoped to be I remember routinely making the trip whenever I could manage it because it was so much fun just to be able to play. Not to mention that downtown Naples was a blast! For a teenager without a vehicle it was merely a matter of catching the right bus.

During the summer I spent countless hours in Pozzuoli at the American beach playing pinball and foosball and occasionally swimming, of course. And watching girls, naturally!

Summer was really fantastic because there was no school to interfere with a reasonably busy teen schedule involving a complete exploration of the area in and around Naples. This is where you find some of the best pizza in the world, mainly because of the aforementioned fresh ingredients, which, when cooked, are safe to eat as well.

The family unit visited Rome on more than one occasion, sometimes just us kids. Nice fountains! What history!

In the fall the football team and company, including the cheerleading squad and the necessary complement of chaperones, boarded a couple of busses and made the trip north to Livorno for the annual game between American schools. I was on the team as a backup and didn't play all that much although I do believe I kicked off once to start a game. I only weighed about 90 pounds at the time and most of the other guys were a lot bigger; say, twice as big.

It didn't take me very long to lose most of my money in an impromptu poker game on the bus.

We managed to upset a few people along the way, first by entertaining the other drivers by 'mooning' them on the way up, but particularly at the leaning Tower of Pisa on our return trip. Apparently some of the coin boxes in the binocular machines around the periphery were relieved of their contents and it turned out that the management was not amused. It created a fairly big row upon our return until the missing funds were anonymously restored! No harm, no foul! But I don't believe we would have been welcomed back at the tower with open arms.

```
In order to measure the infinite one must
oneself be eternal.
    Given the beginning described in the Big
Bang theory, our universe does not meet this
qualification; wherefore no sentient being or
other abstract entity within this realm does
either.
```

Skip ahead to late 1969.

A friend and I decided to avail ourselves of the use of an old motorcycle that had been sitting outside the AFSOUTH gate for as long as we could remember. It didn't appear that anyone ever used this wreck and for all intents and purposes it looked like it had been abandoned there.

In order to start this bike all you had to do was put something in the ignition slot, even a small stick, which is what I think we used.

Come joyride time the bike would of course not start. Water in the gas maybe. We pushed it for some distance trying to jump-start it until at last the engine did catch, at least momentarily, whereupon I jumped on the back and we took off with my buddy at the controls. We went through this fairly exhausting procedure a few times.

We fully intended to return the bike; we were just having some fun, not intending to cause any harm or inconvenience anyone. It seemed like no one ever used it anyway so who would miss it for a few hours?

```
"Think about how stupid the average person
is, then realize that half of them are stupider
than that."
 — George Carlin (1937 - 2008), Comedian
```

I believe we made it all of a couple dozen blocks before we were apprehended by the Carabinieri, who, it turns out, were not entirely happy with us for taking off with the bike. Apparently a concerned citizen had notified the authorities the moment we left. Some people are so touchy!

A very unhappy on-duty officer of the watch at AFSOUTH that day, namely my Dad, picked me up from wherever it was they were holding us and ultimately made an arrangement with the Italian authorities whereupon I was allowed to leave the country without spending any time in an Italian prison as long as I promised not to return any time soon.

Which I did. Quickly! I will spare you the angst of the seething teenage love I was subjected to as I was separated from my one true love, or so it seemed at the time.

Chapter 05

CAREER

I started working upon return to Albuquerque at the tender age of 15 while still in high school. One of the local pancake houses needed a busboy and my sister knew the manager. I jumped at the opportunity! Soon after I was promoted to dishwasher! From there it was only a short walk to being a cook. It wasn't enough to live on but it supplied some spending money.

I originally went to work for the sole purpose of collecting a paycheck to provide the things needed to survive for myself and eventually my family. You know, food, clothing, shelter, transportation, entertainment, that kind of stuff. It was the expected thing to do.

I didn't find out till much later that work has much to offer beyond simply collecting a paycheck. Yes, I admit it, I was young and somewhat naïve. I got over it.

Upon graduation from Highland High School in 1971 I spent an entire year attempting to find meaningful employment. I knew I didn't want to be a short order cook forever. That just isn't where the money is. Finding any such profitable position proved to be impossible, however, as I had none of this thing folks were calling 'experience'.

So I did the next best thing. I volunteered to join the Army on condition they send me to Germany instead of Vietnam.

```
"If you're not failing every now and again,
it's a sign that you're not doing anything very
innovative."
   — Woody Allen (1935 - ), Actor, Writer,
Comedian...
```

It was during this time that I experienced a came-near-death-but-pulled-through-it-experience. This Memorable Event happened during boot camp.

Fort Polk, Louisiana was a big place.

It was common practice to transport the troops in what we affectionately called cattle cars; i.e. a big rig 18-wheeler hauling an enclosed semi-trailer with venting just above the benches running along the length of each side. I was the last man on board one morning and ended up standing just inside the rear double doors which were swung closed and supposedly latched on the outside to prevent them from swinging open during the trip.

And off we went to the rifle range.

The door behind me seemed solid enough, more like a wall. Leaning against it to brace myself against the swaying motion of the trailer may not have been the brightest thing I ever did but at the time it didn't seem like all that bad an idea since there wasn't anywhere to sit; we were that crowded.

Well, I learned about Murphy's Law long after this, but sure enough, as chance would have it, the latch chose this moment to behave most unlatchly. The forward acceleration of the truck combined with my leaning on it was all it took for the huge door to swing silently open on well-oiled hinges.

One moment I'm leaning on a wall and in the next moment there's nothing but air behind me. I admit it came as something of a surprise.

Twenty feet behind us was another identical truck and each behemoth was moving down the road at about 45 MPH. Even if the fall didn't kill me the truck behind us would surely have been unable to avoid running me over.

My leaning position continued its inexorable directional motion in a manner that I am quite sure could be very accurately described by all three of Newton's Laws of Motion as I began the short trip to the road surface.

I still can only explain what happened next with barely disguised incredulity.

The passage of Time slowed tremendously for me. Fractions of seconds became seconds. I kid you not. Everything began happening in super slow motion, at least from my perspective.

```
Excerpt from Missygirl the Calico Cat Book
of Daily Quotes:

Our perception of the speed of passing moments
is based almost entirely on electro-chemical
reactions deep inside our brain. I say almost
because we can't rule out the very thing we are
measuring as being a factor in the equation.

This perception can be altered by changing the
make-up of the chemicals and/or the speed of
the electrical impulse. The brain can do this
all by itself given a natural stimulus such as
fear and of course this effect can be induced
```

using artificial stimuli.

This tells us two things:
1) Time goes by only as fast as we think it does.
2) We don't really know if Time has a speed of its own or how we would go about measuring it.

It may seem obvious that Time stands still for no one but there really is no way to actually prove this just yet.

    I took advantage of this strange time dilation circumstance to carefully look around whereupon I espied a floor-to-ceiling aluminum pole within reach on my left. With literally no time to spare, as I fell out the back of that truck, I extended my left arm and unerringly grasped that pole in a grip so tight it dented the metal.

    In the next moment I was dangling by one hand with my feet just inches above the surface of the road flashing by beneath us.

    The truck driver behind us laid on his horn and began decelerating.

    I wasn't about to let go of that pole but the guys nearest me formed an unbreakable chain of arms that reached out and hauled me back into the trailer as our own driver began slowing down. It took some few moments for Time as I knew it to begin resuming its normal pace.

    This kind of experience will leave you marked, let me tell you. One is invariably reminded of just how precious each moment really is. I still believe to this day that I am living on borrowed time.

    I eventually completed basic training but not with my original unit.

My lungs became badly infected and I ended up in the base hospital for some weeks. This was the kind of hospital where instead of laying about all the time you were expected to get up and help out with the cleaning. When the doctors released me I was unable to rejoin my original company because I had missed too much training. I was put in a new company which had advanced to about the point where I had left off.

I was given a used M16 rifle that had not been properly centered and I couldn't hit the broad side of a barn with it. I nearly flunked the rifle range test. Actually, I think I did flunk, but the Sergeant gave me a break when I explained what the situation was: that it was actually the fault of the rifle that no amount of compensation could overcome, which really was true. He couldn't hit the broad side of a barn with it either and sent me on my way. I never did fire a rifle again although I did once carry one during an exercise.

Basic training over, I was ordered to proceed to Fort Benjamin Harrison in Indianapolis for, what did they call it? Oh, yes: advanced individual training (or AIT). The Army decided to take advantage of the fact that I am an expert typist and put me in the stenographer training program.

This program was four months of very intensive stuff under one very intensive older female instructor and I say that with all appropriate fondness and due respect. She routinely cracked the whip over her students and she got results! She could teach! Learning Gregg shorthand, which I have never once used afterwards since the colonel refused to dictate, was an interesting mental exercise at the very least, but under her tutelage it became as easy as buttering your toast. It became second nature to write as fast as people talk.

After graduating in what amounted to a tie for first in class, which I confess to in all due modesty because the competition was fierce, and as a reward getting promoted to SPEC4, I returned to Albuquerque for 30 days of well-deserved R&R before departing for my duty post. I was ordered to report to Nellingen, Germany, near Stuttgart, where I was put to work as an office boy doing typing for the general staff.

Germany was a real hoot. I had some of the best times of my life once again. Nevertheless the rigidity of the Army way of life did not mesh well with my free-spirited philosophy and it soon became apparent that three years was long enough to be a soldier.

Fast forward to my honorable discharge in New Jersey some 27 months later. With an Army Commendation Medal to boot. And one ruptured eardrum received on the flight back when I inadvertently fell asleep on the plane.

I had made it back to The World once again. Word to the wise and note to self: do not fall asleep on trans-Atlantic flights if one's ears do not 'pop' by themselves.

I was unemployed for a while after leaving the service.

One of the first jobs I was able to find involved unloading thousands of plants from the trailer of a semi-truck for a local nursery. This job lasted an entire day. And frankly, I'm surprised I made it through the whole day.

I eventually ended up with a job as a typesetter at a local newspaper, again owing to my deftness at the keyboard, all thanks to a natural talent and one fine teacher known as Mr. Douglas, who ran the best typing class anywhere during my time in high school in Naples.

It proved to be a dead end job but it served its purpose, mainly by impressing upon me the strong desire to avoid such a job in the future.

```
"I'm an old newspaper man myself, but I quit
because I found out there was no money in old
newspapers".
  — Jack Benny (1894 - 1974), Comedian, Actor
```

There was a gentleman that came in to fix our primitive typesetting computer on a fairly regular basis because it broke down all the time. We usually found time to chat because much of his time was spent in waiting for some task to complete while I set my own schedule when working this graveyard shift. There wasn't anyone else around and once the work was done my time was my own although I did have to wait to clock out. When he told me how much his job paid, about ten times more than my own, I knew that I was definitely in the wrong profession.

I returned to school full time using my GI benefits; 'technical' school to be precise.

After switching to the IT industry from the 'you are going nowhere' industry I was actually able to begin looking forward to the 'solving challenges at work' phase and gaining satisfaction from a job well done. It was no longer just about collecting a paycheck although getting a bigger one sure helped my growing family and was of course a nice to have that I had to have. I actually liked what I was doing. One of the lucky few I suppose.

```
  Time, space and gravity are
```
dimensional
```
 effects,
meaning they are extra-universal in nature.
This should tell us something.
```

Ultimately I spent almost twenty-nine years working diligently as a mainframe system software designer, developer, programmer, debugger, analyst, you name it and I did it, in pretty much any computer language; the last eighteen years at a large software company near Detroit.

We had two basic kinds of work, new development and maintenance of existing systems. Each has its own set of disciplines, both very interesting.

Maintenance means changing existing code to fix an error or to improve performance and has to be done very carefully indeed. The real trick to changing existing code is in not creating any bugs in the process.

Eighteen years is a long time to stay at one company in the IT industry but this was actually not unusual at the company I joined in 1989, which is now in Detroit. There were (and still are) quite a few dedicated individuals a lot smarter than I who stayed put as long or longer.

The right technical environment combined with good pay, good people and interesting challenges as well as access to the latest technological advances and language translators was the big attraction.

It was the right place for a programmer to be: in a company whose business was selling software, as opposed to a company that used computer systems to perform their core processes but this wasn't their real business, like insurance or banking or manufacturing.

We had to be bleeding edge because we wrote the code. We had to have everything our clients did, which was pretty much every programming language currently in use on the planet and the systems they run on.

```
"If a word in the dictionary were misspelled,
how would we know?"
    — Steven Wright (1955 - ), Comedian
```

I worked on a team supporting a mainframe product bringing many millions of dollars into the company annually.

At first I fixed bugs for them and in the process created many more. Not always but often enough. It couldn't be helped, it was the nature of the beast. There wasn't any way to fully test changes throughout the entire million-line system that was our product. I quickly grew weary of fixing bugs I had created. I knew there had to be a better way.

I went about inventing an entirely new QA system used for *completely* automated testing of batch (running in the background) applications. The ability to play scripts and check results without human intervention was an unprecedented advance. This methodology was so successful I tasked myself to create the same capability for online applications, those systems that run in the foreground, sometimes called 'interactive'.

Whole teams of developers *had* been spending time manually testing scripts and generally not catching all sorts of problems. With the advent of my new automated testing systems these nice folks were freed up to focus full time on what they were really good at and this was decidedly *not* testing or recording scripts.

Where once only a few hundred scripts could be checked using whole teams of people and many weeks of effort, now thousands of scripts could be verified overnight with only one person checking summary results.

This new technology was entirely my own epiphany and creation. Which is to say I thought of it, designed it, coded it and installed it. I also documented it quite thoroughly. And yes, I borrowed heavily from off the shelf products to get the job done. Standardization using other permanent solutions was a key element of the design process.

What had been a nightmare of human effort and coordination

Insufferable Indifference - The Mocking of America

became an administrative process that semi-non-technical folks could handle without knowing anything at all about the software they were testing.

What I offered these folks was revolutionary if I say so myself. Systems providing true automated testing as opposed to people trying to do everything manually! What a concept!

These systems took away all the drudgery of the testing process and provided the ability for 100% code coverage.

The impact this new process had on my team was dramatic! Product quality became virtually guaranteed! Developers now had time to deal with the real work for their pay grade while testing was mostly delegated to others, as it should be.

Some developers used this time they previously didn't have to invent and patent their own unique ideas. The dynamic ripples spreading out from the testing systems I had implemented were many and far reaching, all good for the company and the people working there.

You could say that my new automated testing systems cascaded through the division to other products because they did. I know they did because once management saw the excellent results we had achieved on our own team I was asked to implement these systems for all other product lines.

So it was that I created a relatively generic test platform that pretty much any team could tap into for automatically testing their product to achieve the same rock-solid test results my own team was enjoying. Over time this new testing methodology saved many, many, many millions of dollars in company funds when compared to the way things had been done previously. I say with all due modesty that, over time, these savings could easily surpass the 50 million dollar mark.

I was glad to have the opportunity to do what I did and I'm glad my ideas were so useful. The company even incorporated my concepts into a salable product although I lost track of where that went.

I had actually hoped I would be given slightly more than a pat on the back along with the ritual "Atta Boy" for doing this wonderful work but it didn't turn out that way. It really was no surprise when I was told to be happy to still have a job, a well-paying job at that, although it did not pay nearly as much as I had hoped it would.

So, a word to the wise. If you have a really good idea involving saving or making money but you have signed a contract stating that all your work belongs to someone else in return for a steady paycheck, if at all possible, keep it to yourself until you have a chance to pursue it on your own. Otherwise plan on cheerfully donating it for the cause. Which is how I try to think about it.

There can never be just one moment.

There can be zero moments as in a theoretical null universe or more than one moment as in our universe but there can never be just one moment by itself.

Any given moment has a previous moment and is followed by a next moment. This is the inalterable nature of Time.

Furthermore, any given moment can be divided into immeasurable sub-moments.

Hence we observe infinity going in both directions.

Staying fairly healthy most of the time, if ever I did get sick I really got sick and was usually down and out for a week or better. I normally had the kind of job that offered sick time to cover those days (or weeks) when I was unable to work which definitely helped to smooth over those infrequent rough patches. Except for one occasion:

My first IT job, which I started prior to my actual graduation from technical school, was doing software maintenance as the rep for a consulting firm helping an oil company in Borger, Texas. It lasted all of nine months before I was afflicted with Hepatitis. After all those years in Italy avoiding it I had to catch it now. Darn near killed me. The doctor said I could not work for at least eight weeks, maybe twelve, maybe sixteen.

That was the end of that job. They had a 'no work, no pay' policy that I had agreed to in writing before starting in their employ. I suppose I could have returned to this position once my recovery was complete, assuming it was still open. I never did find out.

I returned to Albuquerque "to recover amongst family and friends" and eventually started programming at the UNM IT center, a job I held only two years because the pay was obscenely low, true technical challenges were minimal, and I knew I could do better.

And indeed I did, first in Connecticut, then in Michigan.

My professional career really took off after this, almost ended again years later due to a weird allergy condition, and then took off again. It has been a wild ride.

```
Time did not begin at the moment of the Big
Bang since a 'moment' is a unit of Time and
you can't have a moment that hasn't yet been
created.  Time clearly existed prior to any
bang.
```

When you begin working you will discover that large sums of money will be 'withheld' from each paycheck for 'payroll taxes'. Other big sums will be 'deducted' for 'social programs'. The difference between 'deducting' and 'withholding' appears to be in who collects these funds although to tell the truth it made little difference to me what you called it, my paycheck was still substantially smaller, on the order of thirty to forty percent smaller.

```
"The hardest thing in the world to understand
is the income tax."
 — Albert Einstein (1879 - 1955), Physicist
```

I never really minded paying these taxes because as far as I knew everyone else was doing the same thing and having the SSA disability insurance as a reputed cushion to fall back on in time of need gave me at least a somewhat reassuring feeling if nothing else. Besides, my grandparents were receiving SSA checks and helping keep these trust funds solvent seemed like a good idea.

This went on for over thirty five years, and again, like most of you, I lived paycheck to paycheck all this time. And yes, in hindsight, if I had done things even just a little bit differently I might be far more money rich today.

But this was not to be.

And money rich does not necessarily equate to 'everything is right'.

Chapter 06

CAREER TURNING POINT

2003 was the year I turned fifty. Two cars 'accidents' and two major surgeries on my spine put me on the sidelines for most of the year.

The first (not at fault) car incident occurred near the end of January.

Someone, with child in car, was in a hurry to get home with their fried chicken and came shooting out of a driveway only to clip the right rear side of the car I was driving along in at 45 miles per hour. Got spun around pretty good, all 180 degrees, and real quick like.

I walked away thinking how lucky no one had been injured. The car was a goner.

Two weeks later I knew different. That was when the pain began in earnest.

I saw a great variety of doctors over the next few months until finally being referred to a young spinal surgeon who examined some images of my spine and told me I "needed his help". Said I needed "spinal fusion". "Minimally invasive" spinal surgery was scheduled in April. He went in through the front of my neck and attached some kind of clamp and screw arrangement on my spine at the C7 / T1 junction.

I was 'cleared' to return to work sometime in June, basically against my wishes as I did not feel ready and indeed this did not go at all well. I had been recovering quite slowly and still had great trouble moving about because of the extreme pain I was experiencing in the neck, back and shoulder area. I was taking heavy duty doses of morphine and dealing with the side effects of this horrible regimen.

Near the end of June the second car incident occurred. Not at fault again. And no, I was not all doped out on Morphine.

I was moving down the right turn lane nearing an intersection with a red light. Some young driver tried to cut left through an opening in the line of waiting traffic where some idiot had left a gap. This driver was trying to get into the driveway coming up on my right just before the intersection.

The driver moved quickly. Very quickly. But not quick enough. And neither could I stop quickly enough before slamming into the passenger side of the other driver's car. Even though I was half-anticipating such a maneuver, having spotted the gap and having slowed down accordingly, I was still moving too fast to avoid colliding with the car that came shooting across in front of me in a mad dash for the driveway entrance.

Both cars sustained major damage. Didn't do me any good either. I don't believe the other driver was injured although I am fairly sure this person was surprised by the appearance of my car at just precisely the wrong moment.

This individual later tried to convince the traffic court that I had caused the whole thing because I was 'in a hurry'.

The traffic court judge was not swayed by this argument since it was this person who turned in front of me precipitating our unfortunate collision, and besides, I was not in a hurry; I was on my way to a physical therapy session and I tended to drive a lot slower and more defensively since I was still recovering from the first incident.

I believe I was still wearing that awful neck collar! Thank goodness!

My spinal surgeon, upon reexamination, declared that I was once again fully disabled. The fusion was not 'taking'.

More surgery followed in September, this time much more aggressive in nature than the April surgery. This time he went in through my back and left a very large scar. I believe an additional rod, clamp and screws were placed in the same location as in the first operation. Or more likely it was a replacement setup. I never did find out.

I came to with a tube poking out of my back and in an incredible amount of pain, virtually unbearable. To add insult to injury, the hospital staff refused to give me adequate sedatives those first few days. Doctor's orders, apparently.

I was left in a condition that I would not wish on anyone else.

```
"Isn't it a bit unnerving that doctors call
what they do 'practice'?"
    — George Carlin (1937 - 2008), Comedian
```

The fairly graphic description of this condition which immediately follows this explanation is presented to you purely for the sake of accuracy. Again, no sympathy is asked for or required, it's only record keeping, so please, let us have none of that.

What I can only refer to as permanent nerve damage leaves me feeling *continuous* exquisitely severe pain right between my shoulder blades, right where I can't reach it, the proverbial itch that cannot be scratched. It is not just one spot although the root of it is just that, a regular little fireball at the center of my being. It spreads from this central spot of *continuous* agony to deleteriously affect my back, neck and shoulder muscles, depending on my level of activity.

The concept that I have a bad implant has recently been raised as a possibility. You can just bet I will be checking into this avenue of investigation. Maybe I can be fixed after all! It is always good to dream of what could be.

This is not chronic pain, it is *persistent* pain.

It exists as a presence within living a life all its own. This presence tends to redirect one's thoughts whether one wishes this or not. Given the old 1-10 pain scale and placing most people at zero, I now live life at level 6 to 10 full time. Day and night. Going on ten years now. With no way to prove it. No such test. Lucky me.

```
Time and Space are not Products of Creation.
They are Ingredients.
    I say Time and Space because while they do
seem to be inextricably interwoven they clearly
are not the same thing.
    These two manifestations exist independently
of one another. Infinity gives them a strong
common bond, an understanding if you will, that
allows them to work together seamlessly. Aside
from this they have nothing else in common.
```

I look reasonably normal but as you know appearances can be very deceiving. No medical tests can conclusively pinpoint my physical situation to any degree. The area in question is all hidden by clamps, rods and screws so imaging technology cannot really 'see' anything anymore.

The doctor has my word alone, along with a large scar along my spine and oversize 'muscular' shoulders as if I lifted weights (not). My neck size has increased from 17 to 20 inches all thanks to muscle spasms.

There really is no way to describe to you what it feels like to be in this much perpetual pain. It would be like trying to put into words what unending sexual climax feels like. You just have to be there. Here is my best shot:

There is this unbelievably nasty thing living right between my shoulder blades right where I can't reach it. This incredibly burning / itching / stinging sensation rotates and twists at will, often masking an underlying supremely sore ache in the spine, leaving the entire area extremely tender and sore. This constantly disturbing sensation makes everything difficult, especially breathing but also moving and such like becomes cumulatively and additively difficult as each day progresses.

The muscles in the area can spasm repeatedly and continuously until they too become exceedingly painful, sometimes feeling like a hot iron bar laying across the shoulders. At its worst the pain is paralyzing, which, thankfully, has only happened once; Thanksgiving again, 2009. More about this later.

I think of it as internal pain and external pain.

The external pain I can mitigate just slightly through massage and hot showers.

The internal pain is beyond belief, affecting breathing, eating and especially sleeping. I no longer sleep, I only fade out briefly, then back to my new reality, perhaps an hour or two at best. Makes it hard to focus though not impossible.

I say my condition is odd because while persistent pain does disrupt my thinking in general and is in fact quite disturbing and bothersome, it doesn't prevent me from thinking altogether, and in point of fact seems to have improved my cogitational abilities to some degree.

The kind of technical work I was engaged in required the ability to concentrate on thousands or even millions of lines of code 'all at once' over long periods of time; hours anyway, sometimes days. Losing this capability actually sharpened my focus. I *have* to get more done in less time because I am only operational for short periods of time. Combine this with the pressing need to think about something other than the pain and what you get is a more finely focused thinking process confined to very limited timeframes.

You may be wondering: if I am in such bad pain how could I possibly write a book like this? Or any book?

A little bit at a time, that's how. Only with the greatest of difficulty, that's how.

But mainly I am able to pen these particular words because my annoyance at those who have unnecessarily f'ed with my life greatly exceeds my legendary patience and I do not intend to let them get away with it scot-free. Not anymore. Enough is enough.

I am sure it is hard for you to imagine or even believe that any activity, any movement, increases the level of pain I experience, incrementally and cumulatively, until it becomes unbearable and I have to lay down and focus on relaxing, but this is exactly what happens.

Just plain old normal activities ratchet up the flame! Breathing, talking, walking, driving, sitting and typing at a keyboard, all the things I used to do without thinking about it, all of a sudden take on a new significance as instruments of torture. The more I do the more it hurts. Strange, but true. Coughing and sneezing are particularly onerous now!

The only way to minimize my pain is to be in full control of my daily activities.

In addition to having more needles than any one person should ever have to have stuck in their back in one lifetime being stuck into mine on a regular basis, I actually ingested increasingly high levels of morphine sulfate by pill for a consecutive period of time exceeding seven years before deciding to switch doctors after Dr. H recommended surgically implanting a 'pump' that would dispense the morphine "more better". The morphine was slowly killing me and I wanted less, not more.

```
"Your pain is the breaking of the shell that
encloses your understanding."
— Kahlil Gibran (1883 - 1931), Philosopher,
Poet, Writer
```

Dr. E helped me stop taking morphine altogether by putting me on a decreasing dose over a period of months. I quit using the 'easy' way. The fact that I disliked taking it intensely because of the negative impact it was having on my body and mind was certainly helpful. Dr. E persuaded me that the body generates its own supply of pain suppressant chemicals given the chance, at least to some degree, and that artificial pain meds like morphine interfere with the body's natural ability to do this.

Turns out he is right. After the initial artificial short-term pain 'reduction' the morphine actually served to increase the level of pain. I can testify to the truth of this because I lived through it to tell the tale you now hold in your hands.

The only reason I am not rolling around on the floor moaning in agony, the only reason I have not been driven stark raving mad by the pain I experience from moment to moment has something to do with my ancestry, my upbringing and the fact that I choose when to rest. Only by resting whenever I determine this is necessary can I have any kind of effect on the intensity of the pain.

The difference between 6 and 10 on the pain scale is an exponential difference. Believe it or not.

I am blessed with a high level of patience and I have very strong willpower. I stubbornly hang on to a fighting spirit that refuses to give in even while the pain affects me in ways over which I have no control.

I can no longer focus properly for any extended length of time. I can no longer produce the same amount or quality of technical work I once was able to produce in a career spanning over 28 years in the IT industry. I just can't focus that way anymore.

I did try.

After missing almost the entire year of 2003 due to the automobile incidents and surgery related disabilities, I attempted to return to work.

I spent the next four years attempting to return to work.

I did in fact produce some of my best technical work (the aforementioned QA systems matured into testing platforms during this time) despite being unable to work full time. I guess I was trying to compensate for the hours I was missing, still wanted to do my part for king and country, still be a productive employee and carry on as if nothing were wrong or different, which ultimately proved to be impossible.

I could only work part time. My condition would allow for nothing else. But the company still considered me a full-time employee and I continued receiving full pay and benefits.

My co-workers were not too happy about this. Work related accusations regarding unauthorized changes to production systems began to fly. None of it was true. Didn't matter. People began acting differently towards me, as if I were some sort of unavoidable antagonism.

At one point I was escorted to the door and told not to return until I had sign-off from some kind of counselor. Apparently I had mental health issues I was unaware of that needed to be explained to me. This was my reward for walking out of an unproductive meeting.

It was nice to have mandatory paid time off for a few weeks, but it didn't take the counselor that long to determine I was as normal as anyone else, albeit with a relatively unique physical problem, and I was given permission to rejoin the workforce, which by this time I wasn't really sure I wanted to do but felt as if I had no choice in the matter. Still had to put food on the table and all, you know, pretend normality.

The company so valued my expertise that they kept me on the payroll for these four years before informing me in no uncertain terms that I must put in the hours, 'be normal' (like everyone else) "or else".

Dr. H had recently informed me that he, and I quote, "couldn't believe I was still working".

With little choice in the matter I accepted forced retirement in April 2008 with a greatly reduced but still substantial paycheck provided by a major disability insurer with the requirement to 're-document' my (permanent) disability condition each year or face discontinuance of benefits; the policy provides for payments to cease when I turn 65.

I wasn't exactly happy about it but what could I do?

Completely unaware of the rude awakening I was in store for, I initiated what I assumed would be a fairly routine application process for SSA disability benefits. You know, the payments you are supposed to get if you become disabled and can't work full time anymore?

The first clue that something was not quite right was when it became apparent that hiring a good attorney is virtually mandatory if you want any chance at all of actually receiving a favorable response from this monolithic enterprise.

5%. This value is the current estimate of our share of the universe, the matter and energy that we can see, every particle everywhere. The other 95% is undetectable by direct observation at our current level of technology although we can see normal matter and light being affected by this unseen stuff. Consequently we have no real idea exactly what it is.

Nevertheless we have theoretically gauged relative attributes and percentages and even assigned names to this invisible stuff which seems to be acting like scaffolding for 'ordinary' matter. Dark Energy is estimated to occupy 71% and Dark Matter the other 24%.

Good to know.

Chapter 07

DISABILITY DENIED!

More than five years have passed since I first filed the necessary papers for the purpose of collecting disability benefits from the Social Security Administration and so far I have not collected dime one. I *am* disabled but not considered so by these champions of society's virtues.

I collect private disability insurance benefit payments because I can no longer do the job I was doing when I was Struck Down by Unfortunate Circumstances and the insurance company believes what my doctor is telling them.

SSA disability insurance benefit collection requirements appear to mandate the inability to work at *any* job. This establishes a slightly different standard, although, frankly, there really is no job I can do satisfactorily, even 'greeter' would be problematic, and I doubt the pay would be anything like what I used to make.

I have been hung out to dry, left in limbo so to speak, living on fixed payments from private disability insurance with no guarantee of renewal, with no medical, dental or hospitalization coverage other than what I can find in my own pocket, unable to leave my present location because this is where my doctors are and this is where my 'case' is pending, waiting on some government bureaucrat to decide the fate of myself and my family as well since I am the sole provider.

I have been trying to figure out, after being on 'permanent' disability for five years now, what I am supposed to do if the ever-so-knowledgeable folks at the SSA ultimately decide on a more or less permanent unchallengeable basis that they do not consider me a qualified candidate for SSA disability benefits, for whatever reasons they choose to use, and if so, what exactly am I supposed to do, try to re-enter the job market? What do I say to prospective employers? Maybe something like this:

"Hello, I would appreciate a job, any job. Please ignore the fact that I have been on permanent disability these last five years. Please ignore the fact that I can't work full time. I require a salary in excess of six figures. Thank you for your consideration."

It doesn't seem to me like this would go over very well at any company I ever heard of.

The treatment I have received at the hands of the SSA thus far has been reprehensible at best and unbelievably incompetent at worst. I would even go so far as to call it sanctioned criminal negligence.

Sour grapes? Not at all. Mad as hell? You bet!

I ran smack into a wall of Insufferable Indifference. If not for the private group disability insurance policy I had with my former employer my family and I would long ago have been homeless, perhaps far worse.

Everyone should know what to expect should one become unlucky enough to become disabled in these United States of America but cannot get the ignoramuses at the SSA (which reads better backwards) to agree with this diagnosis. Apparently this happens some 50% of the time from what I see on the internet, not a very good track record, and making for a very lucrative legal practice for some.

Insufferable Indifference - The Mocking of America

Who knew there were so many fakers in America? Who knew there was such a monster disability fraud problem in this country that an entire federal administration of many, many thousands of people would be engaged in and devoted to rooting out this evil and in so doing routinely deny benefits to all those folks who actually need them as well?

```
Excerpt from Missygirl the Calico Cat Book
of Daily Quotes:
Exponential growth of any given problem is
easily achieved simply by ignoring it.
```

What we have here is what I call a 'negative' system, one in which you are automatically considered a liar and a cheat who must clear multiples hurdles placed in your way and 'prove' conclusively that you are in fact as bad off as you say you are. And you must do all this while you are in fact as bad off as you say you are. Not an easy task.

You can't penalize everyone because of the transgressions of the few. Instead, go after the few.

The story goes like this:

You file for disability benefits. Then you wait. And wait. And wait. Eventually more information is demanded, not requested, information that will basically be ignored but apparently is something they are required to ask for anyway.

You will almost certainly be sent a notice to appear before a doctor of their choosing. Noncompliance with this directive will almost certainly result in an automatic negative decision on your application. Here's how they word it on the form verbatim, bold letters are theirs:

"If you fail to keep this appointment, the decision will be based on the evidence now in file which may result in a denial or cessation of benefits."

A 'hearing' is scheduled so a 'judge' can determine if in fact you have a credible reason for requesting disability benefits. It doesn't really matter what your own doctor has to say. It doesn't really matter what you have to say. Your case will almost certainly be decided independent of these sources of information. Mine was.

Somewhere between eighteen months and 2½ years after filing for disability benefits, I can't recall exactly how long it took, the SSA agreed to do me the favor of giving me an 'expedited' hearing by means of flying in a 'judge' from California. The written decision he handed down long afterwards was unexpected to say the least.

Apparently I was not disabled because, among other things, I actually showed up for and sat through the mandatory hearing, proving right then and there that nothing was wrong with me. Additional evidence of my non-disabled status was my demonstrated ability to repeatedly lift an 8 ounce bottle of water.

I am not going to say this person out-and-out laughed at me but the amount of time he spent giggling to himself did strike me as being rather peculiar. I never did see any humor in the proceedings.

The negative decision this judge ultimately issued was based completely on the opinion of some 'medical expert' who briefly reviewed my files but never actually saw me in person.

The judge applied 'weight' to the position opined by his in-house expert and gave no weight to anything I or my doctor had to say.

A U.S. district court judge later deemed this 'decision' invalid. See:

Government Print Office (GPO) 10-14983 - CLEMENT V.

SOCIAL SECURITY, COMMISSIONER OF

These people call themselves judges although I don't believe I have ever seen any elections giving them this status. I have no idea as to their true qualifications for this title nor are they forthcoming in providing any of this information.

After my most recent hearing on 8 January 2013 I called their office to inquire as to the spelling of the name of the 'judge' I had seen earlier that day. I know it was something like 'Sesame' and I needed the exact spelling.

"I cannot tell you this. I cannot give you any information." was the only thing the receptionist was able to say, repeatedly; like a broken record, like she was practicing to be the best at being able to say this, because it was part of her job description and she wanted to get good marks in the Useless Customer Interactions category.

Real helpful folks! I'm not real sure why they even bother to answer the phone.

The activities of these people are shrouded in secrecy.

I find it more than passing strange that they have armed guards to search all visitors prior to allowing entry to the SSA office and what appeared to be bullet proof glass for the receptionist while our schools do not enjoy this same privilege. Apparently, to judge by appearances, these brave civil servants are under constant threat of some kind thus requiring more protection than you or I can reasonably expect in our day to day activities.

I saw nothing of value during my most recent visit, just a few empty offices. Are these people truly in constant fear for their lives or is this just unnecessary posturing of some sort? From whom do they fear attack? What kind of reprisal do they expect? And for what?

Could it be that screwing over the American public is a dangerous occupation?

Any system with parameters of this nature is fundamentally flawed and would normally self-destruct if left on its own. In this case the 'system' is artificially supported using your money, a lot of it.

These so-called 'judges' are nothing of the sort. They do not represent justice. They represent the best interests of the SSA and nothing more. They are employees. To them it is just a job. They have no cares about you or your problems, this is not what they are paid to do. They are lackeys of the SSA and they do what they are told to do. And apparently what they are told to do is to deny 'benefits' to *everyone* and especially if the claimant refuses to see an SSA selected doctor, as I did for almost five years on orders from my attorney.

Excerpt from *Missygirl the Calico Cat Book of Daily Quotes*:

```
Wisdom comes only to those who know enough
to know they don't have any.
```

A favorite tactic of the SSA is to require you to see a doctor of their choosing. It seems certain that the job of this individual is to find reasons to discount your claim that you do indeed have the disability you claim to have, despite the fact that you may already have one or more other doctors who have already validated your condition, which is why you are in this position in the first place.

Do not expect this doctor to have any sympathy for you or your condition. His or her specialty may have nothing at all to do with what is wrong with you; in other words this individual may have little or no expertise at all as to your specific condition. This doctor is paid by the SSA and is therefore necessarily biased in favor of the paymaster. How much honesty can you really expect from such a 'got a good reason to be biased' individual? How much justice can you expect from such a system? My experience says "not much".

My attorney refused to permit me to see an SSA doctor. His reasoning was twofold. First, that the records supplied by my own medical team should be sufficient evidence. Second, no evidence is better than any evidence produced by an SSA appointed doctor.

I had been seeing Dr. H monthly for over seven years and had his affidavit as to my disabled condition. Dr. E, my current treating physician, who currently recertifies my disabled condition with my private disability insurance company each year, is on the list as one of the best doctors in America. Of what true value would a third opinion be? From a stranger?

How can any one individual accurately determine my condition after only a short exam all the while ignoring ten years of medical history? Why would this person's opinion be given any more weight than the considerable weight that should be given the opinion of my own doctors? Does the SSA think my doctors are incompetent? Untrustworthy? Apparently so.

After five years of constant denial, after a federal court judge (a real judge) so much as 'told' the SSA to discard all prior decisions and give more 'weight' to the treating physician's sworn testimony, which would necessarily mean finding in my favor and granting dispensation of my benefits; despite having two experts in my corner, one of whom is rated among the best in America at what he does; despite having ten years of accumulated medical records evidence; the 'judge' at my most recent hearing in January 'ordered' that I see an SSA selected doctor for unspecified "more medical information".

The 'judge' is apparently not sure what to think. And herein lies the crux of the issue. What this person thinks about me seems to be more significant than any amount of medical history or recorded professional opinions. This is so wrong in so many ways.

What does it matter what this person thinks when I have indisputable long term medical evidence as to my true physical condition? How can this 'system' continue to deny the (self-evident) truth after being berated in such a manner by the federal court opinion for acting so stupidly?

In the January 2013 hearing I was kept waiting an hour before being ushered into a mock courtroom containing three people, his honor and two other people. I was required to answer a series of basically irrelevant questions about myself and my daily activities.

I find nothing honorable or even reasonable in this process. It is a sham. Nothing conclusive can possibly be determined in such a setting except that it is possible for a courtroom setting to make people very uncomfortable, to make them feel like they are on trial, that they stand accused of some unknown criminal activity and there is no jury.

February began with receipt of a **NOTICE OF DISABILITY EXAMINATION** form in the mail (their bolding, not mine) from the State of Michigan, Department of Human Services, **DISABILITY DETERMINATION SERVICE FOR SOCIAL SECURITY CLAIMS,** informing me that I must submit myself for inspection like some common barn animal by a doctor of their choosing. All the arrangements had been made for me. All I had to do was show up. In two weeks. An hour's drive away. Transportation not provided.

Why? After all this time? After almost five years of refusing to see a doctor of their choosing, as is my privilege. I called my (new) attorney to inquire. "Because the judge has ordered it" says he.

Apparently there is no choice in the matter when the judge orders it be done.

Why must I be forced to submit to yet another indignation? An 'exam' by an unknown physician, however short or long, can prove nothing one way or another. My condition cannot be accurately diagnosed in this manner. 'Pain' is not anything that can be measured except by the unfortunate recipient.

```
Excerpt from Missygirl the Calico Cat Book
of Daily Quotes:
    Tomorrow does come.  It just seems like
today.
```

I showed up at the appointed place on time and was grateful to see there were no jackbooted armed thugs waiting to search me. I subjected myself to the indignities of the scheduled exam so that my family would not suffer needlessly in the event I was again rejected for benefits out of hand as it specifically states on the notification to attend can happen for refusing to submit as previously noted.

On arrival my blood pressure and weight were checked and my vision was tested. I was asked to squeeze what I can only term as a grip-o-meter although I am sure this is probably not the real name. Many and varied X-Rays were taken, exposing me to I don't know how many undesirable roentgens. I was then instructed to "Please return to the waiting room. The doctor will call you".

By the simple means of unwillingly overhearing the other attendee's conversations, some if not all of whom were also apparently SSA victims, because they were talking louder than the television in the corner, I was able to deduce they had been waiting almost two hours.

I settled down for what appeared would be quite a long wait only to be surprised half an hour later when I was, strangely enough, called ahead of all the other complainees.

Dr. M seemed like a nice enough fellow.

It was difficult to relate at first because I was mad enough to spit nails and he took this as a sign of hostility. I explained that, no, I was not mad at him personally. I was, however, quite upset with the system and my unjustified treatment by same.

"This started ten years ago?" says the doc semi-incredulously. "And you applied for disability five years ago?" He may have been acting. Hard to tell sometimes.

"I can understand your being frustrated" says he.

"Now there's an understatement" was all I could manage to mumble.

The exam proceeded with less animosity after this. Still difficult though.

We talked a bit more about the circumstances. "Two car accidents and two spinal surgeries in 2003" he notes from the record. "These types of surgeries can go bad now and then".

"Yes", I replied, "in my case very bad".

I didn't have to undress or anything like that. He took a quick look at my two surgical scars just by pulling down my collar and had me bend this way and reach that way. "Where does it hurt?" he wants to know. "My hips", I said. "They're shot". He remained unsurprised at anything I said. He had me lie on my back and tried to move my hips a certain way. My joints refused to cooperate. "Relax" says he. "I am" says I.

One of the last things the doctor did was to look at my teeth. "Let me see your teeth" he says. What am I, a horse? I guess my livestock allusion was not too far off the mark after all.

These are the people responsible for deciding my fate and undoubtedly that of many thousands of others? Why? Doesn't seem right somehow.

One can even find ratings of the various 'judges' online, their approval/disapproval ratio, and it generally seems to run about 50%, which is completely outrageous!

The actions of the SSA and their minions in handling my case has been disingenuous at best and entirely abusive at worst. These people are making decisions they shouldn't be making in the first place, based not on reality, not by fairly judging the evidence at hand, but based on the way they feel, and mostly based on what they are told to do by their masters. They choose to conveniently ignore relevant facts in the existing medical record while giving too much 'weight' to irrelevant 'facts' of their own invention such as those established by doctors of their own choosing during an impromptu 30-minute exam.

I have two doctors, both certified in the subspecialty of pain management, and both have certified that I am disabled and cannot work full time.

Seen monthly for over seven years, my first doctor is an anesthesiologist by trade and is very good at what he does. He uses the voluntary medicinal approach, meaning he offers you powerful drugs like morphine "for relief", which, quite frankly, while this may be OK for some folks and does seem to help (a little anyway) short term, ultimately inflicts side effects far worse than the original symptoms ever were.

I followed this philosophy for quite some time, not because I was addicted to morphine, I actually disliked it intensely, but because I was allergic to any alternative 'modern' pain med, as two trips to the emergency room for treatment for life-threatening anaphylactic reactions proved beyond dispute.

My current treating physician believes the body will use its own mechanisms for pain relief if given the chance. He has been rated among the best in America and I believe what he says because I lived through it and he is right.

```
Excerpt from Missygirl the Calico Cat Book
of Daily Quotes:
   If you want to get ahead some things will
have to be left behind.
```

The body generates its own chemical soup based on circumstances. If you override this soup with artificially produced 'man-made' products then the body's own processes never have the opportunity to function properly and can even be radically tainted, leaving an end result of more pain rather than less.

There can be many other major side-effects when using opiate-derived pain medications up to and including death. The brain takes a major hit but it is the internal organs that are affected the most resulting in major systemic effects. Imagine sitting at your desk doing fine one moment only to find in the next that you and your clothing are soaking wet because you are sweating buckets. This is what is known as a 'glandular' problem.

The SSA Disability Insurance Trust Fund does not belong to the government. It belongs to the people who paid in. Repeat. This is not government money. This money is being held in trust for the people, it belongs to the people, and the people should be the ones who decide how it should be administered.

There are enough laws on the books to handle fraudulent transactions. We do not need these SSA minions with their cavalier attitudes deciding for the rest of us who should benefit and who should not. We do not need an entire federal government administration whose sole purpose it is to weed out scofflaws up front using a process that disenfranchises American citizens. We should fire the lot of them. Make them get real jobs like the rest of us. It is the doctors who should be deciding who is and who is not disabled, not some 'judge' in a courtroom setting.

We can re-interview these suddenly unemployed people for the purpose of staffing a federal government administration whose sole purpose would be identifying fraudulent doctors and patients and supplying the evidence to duly elected existing court systems to put them away for good.

If necessary we can enact severe penalties for such behavior, severe enough to discourage just about any doctor from engaging in such practices. Any few remaining unscrupulous individuals attempting such larcenous activity would stick out like the proverbial sore thumb.

I believe we will find that in short order there would be far less fraudulent claims being filed. Without a doctor to certify disability there can be no claim.

The small amount of fraudulent claims on the books should not be nearly enough to bankrupt the system and certainly does not justify the current methodology employed for processing claims.

This approach would also eliminate the need for thousands of attorneys to do battle with the SSA on our behalf.

Chapter 08

THE POSTSCRIPT THAT BECAME A CHAPTER

Bottom line:

1) The representatives of the Social Security Administration deliberately mishandled my claim and in so doing stretched the processing period to an impressive timeframe exceeding five years in duration. This created Unintended Consequences as shown below.

2) It was necessary, with the assistance of a knowledgeable attorney, to petition a federal court to issue a decision *forcing* the SSA to actually review, consider and include in any decision the evidence submitted by myself and my doctors, which, until this was done, they had tacitly declined to do.

On 19 April 2013, five years and two months after filing my SSA disability claim, I received the first indication that my official status had been changed from disabled liar to disabled recipient. I found this out via a voice mail requesting I call a certain individual at the SSA Kansas City Payment Processing Center in order to "answer a few questions so we can finish up this process".

Apparently the judge had ruled in my favor. News to me.

After five long years the SSA finally acquired the good sense to recognize my disability for what it is: a major problem preventing me from working full time.

They have granted me probationary disabled status to remain in effect for three years, after which time a review will be conducted to ascertain if I am in fact still disabled.

This process should never have taken over five years to complete. The back pay amount should never have been allowed to swell so large.

The first judge deliberately and with obvious malice chose to ignore anything I or my doctors had to say about anything and he summarily dismissed my claim with a broad smile on his face. For this I am to be penalized?

Unfortunately this latest ruling cast me from the firing pan into the fire. Here's how:

Earlier I mentioned "hiring a good attorney is virtually mandatory if you want any chance at all of actually receiving a favorable response from this monolithic enterprise". This was way back in Chapter 6. 'Hiring' being the operative word.

What I actually did was retain the services of an SSA disability claim attorney (and the firm he represented) on contingency, meaning he (they) only get paid if the SSA approves my claim. This guy had worked for the SSA and now specialized in helping us normal folk collect our due from his former employer. This attorney eventually moved to Florida to help his Dad whereupon the senior partner took over my case.

Anyhoo, when I spoke with this lady in Kansas City several hours later on this same day she informed me that:

1) she had some money for me, and
2) the judge had signed papers granting 25% of the retroactive

payments to my attorney thereby requiring this amount be withheld from my disbursement.

Whoa, Nelly!

The total retroactive payment amount came to almost $132,000.00, which means the attorney could potentially collect $32,386.25, instead of the $6,000.00 maximum I thought I had agreed to pay more than five years ago contingent on receiving a favorable disability benefit ruling from the SSA.

Let's see now. What did my attorney actually do?

The attorney I first hired retired to Florida about 2½ years into this five-year fiasco after attending one hearing and filing a few briefs electronically. His managing partner took over my case. He too attended one hearing. Let's give them four hours for each 'one-hour' hearing, to include prep time and travel time. Eight hours so far.

Work on two briefs, say eight hours elapsed.

File all motions electronically from the office, say two hours elapsed.

Spend some time on the phone, say four hours elapsed.

Take one deposition, call it two hours.

Total time spent on my case: twenty-four hours.

Assume I am mistaken and double the previous total to arrive at a very generous 48 elapsed work-hours as the maximum amount of time the firm actually spent working on my stuff.

Assume I am still wrong and add 12 hours fudge factor.

Total work time spent doing something related to my case over five years elapsed = 60 hours. One and a half work weeks. Aside from that all they did was wait along with me for the SSA to respond. The amount of work that was done on my behalf could not possibly exceed this amount of time; there just wasn't enough of it, as my circumstances were not actually all that complicated.

This corresponds with a pay scale of $100.00 an hour for their services when you consider the $6,000.00 maximum I thought they would receive if I 'won' my case. How did the contract read? Oh yes, and with *my* emphasis:

"the attorney fee will be calculated as the *lesser* of 25% of retroactive benefits obtained or $6,000.00".

I don't know about you but what this says to me is that the most I will have to give these people is $6,000.00, and I might add that this is not an insignificant amount of money.

The next clause in the contract is the real kicker. It grants them 25% *unconditionally* if 'any additional appeal' is filed on my behalf. The use of the word 'appeal' appears to be fairly open to interpretation here. "Mother may I" is considered an appeal in some circles. In my opinion no additional appeal was filed. The attorney, by his own admission in writing, filed a Complaint with the federal court, not an Appeal.

I was under extreme duress at the time of the signing of the fee agreement. I believe this fact raises the question of the actual legality of signing such a document under such circumstances.

No one in their right mind would agree to give any attorney over $32,000.00 to help them collect SSA disability benefits. No way, no how. That would be insane. Ergo I must not have been in my right mind when I signed the fee agreement.

```
Excerpt from Missygirl the Calico Cat Book
of Daily Quotes:
Where you came from is not nearly as important
as where you are going.
```

Let's recap:

If the SSA permanently denied my claim I would owe the attorney nothing.

If I had been granted disability benefits from day one I would owe the attorney nothing.

If I had been granted disability benefits at the time of the first hearing, 2½ years after I filed the original papers, I would owe the attorney $6,000.00 because at this point in time 25% of retroactive benefits would have been over double this amount and no appeals had been filed.

Now, after being inappropriately delayed for over five years by what I consider to be potentially illegal tactics on the part of the SSA, thus forcing the 'appeal' process (or whatever you want to call it) to run its full course, the attorney fee has swelled to 25% of retroactive benefits, which amount, $32,386.25, was conveniently withheld from my first distribution by the ever so helpful SSA payment center.

Apparently I cannot be trusted to pay my own attorney.

Why is it, I wonder, that the SSA finds it necessary to act on behalf of my attorney?

So, collecting SSA disability benefits when I became disabled not only didn't happen but ended up costing me a small fortune, the equivalent of 14 months' worth of disability benefits.

Now, I am not exactly the most trusting man on the planet. To me this setup stinks to high heaven. I have no proof of any kind except my own experience and I am usually the last to cast aspersions on anyone but it wouldn't really be all that much of a stretch to imagine some kind of hidden subculture feeding at the trough of human suffering here. It all fits quite nicely. *Someone* may be getting rich, very rich, and doing so riding the backs of disabled Americans.

This is retroactive pay we are talking about; *income*, not some kind of special award, not a bonus or a jackpot. These are funds I should have been collecting all along.

Something is fundamentally wrong with this picture when elderly disabled people on a fixed income have to cough up extremely exorbitant attorney fees in order to receive what is rightfully theirs in the first place, and if actually dispensed, is called an *award* when in fact it most definitely is no such thing.

The fact that predatory attorneys are making a (damn good) living preying on the inherent weaknesses to be found in any elderly disabled person is really quite disturbing. At least to me. This type of behavior should in fact be illegal.

Add to this the fact that none of this should have been necessary had the first SSA judge acted more reasonably, i.e. responsibly, instead of ridiculing me while completely ignoring my doctors and the medical record; and that, frankly, $6,000.00 is not only a lot of money for any disabled person on a fixed income to have to pay out-of-pocket to collect SSA disability benefits, it is also more than enough for any such purpose as this.

While I am grateful for the assistance provided by the attorneys I retained in dealing with the unbelievably incompetent SSA during this ordeal, I do not believe they deserve to collect 25% of my retroactive benefits for their services. This is a bit much. Much, much more than I can afford to pay. And much, much more than they earned.

I have asked the judge to reconsider his decision to grant my attorney's firm the fee they have requested but I am not entirely optimistic as to the outcome. It is ultimately up to the judge as to how much the attorney will collect.

```
"Have you ever noticed that the lawyer always
smiles more than the client?"
```

— George Carlin (1937 – 2008), Comedian

The 'Notice of Award' document that I eventually received from the SSA, as if I had won a contest of some kind, while a bit confusing overall, would seem to indicate that I am now eligible for Medicare; only me, not the wife, and if I wish, the medical insurance portion can be retroactively instantiated as well. All I have to do is send a check for $3,496.90.

Let me see if I have this straight. I can pre-activate something I have not been using simply by paying for it. Hmmm. Interesting logic.

Excerpt from *Missygirl the Calico Cat Book of Daily Quotes:*
The only really useful advice is that which comes from within oneself.

My disability stipend is reduced each month by a certain amount in excess of $100.00 to pay a premium into the Medicare system.

Recently I became ill enough to visit my GP for the first time in many years due to another unfortunate life-threatening lung infection.

OK, I'm thinking, I've got Medicare to help me cover the cost!

The doctor's bill I subsequently received was very informative in this regard.

Four line items were listed: office visit, two on-the-spot injections in the good old gluteus maximus and one prescription for antibiotics. Each line item had printed on the line underneath the words: "Medicare Non Allowed", followed by an amount, which I can only (reverse) interpret to mean: Medicare will only pay this amount as the balance was "Non Allowed". For example, Medicare paid a whopping $18.07 of the $130.00 office visit charge. I had to send payment for 71% of the total bill.

I thought it was supposed to be the other way around, with insurance picking up 80%?

And that's not all.

Liberty Mutual Insurance has been paying an extra amount each month to cover the SSA income I would have received had I been granted SSA disability benefits from day one. They did not do this completely out of the goodness of their heart even though this level of goodness is considerable. I do believe they expect to be reimbursed using my retroactive benefits to cover the tab.

The current value of this accumulated 'overpayment' is the SSA monthly disability benefit amount times the 54 months Liberty Mutual has been paying it; somewhere between $120,000.00 and $130,000.00.

Should the attorney firm be allowed to take 25% of the retroactive benefit amount, or any excessive fee amount, well, I think you can do the math.

I sincerely hope the judge does not allow this to happen.

Update:

My attorney has filed a fee petition with the court requesting $21,000.00 as payment for their services. At the same time they sent me a bill for about $1,700.00 to cover their expenses. The expense report looks reasonably accurate, but as I have already pointed out, the fee is excessive and outrageous in the extreme, and if I am going to pay $1,700.00 out of pocket for expenses then these files should be boxed and turned over to me, which I have ordered be done (yes, ordered, not requested, I do not make requests to predatory attorneys), but this has not happened as of yet.

Life in the fast lane.

Three years...

According to the 'Notice of Award', this is the amount of time I have been approved to receive SSA disability benefits, after which time a mandatory review is ordered, giving me the opportunity to do this all over again. Prove I am *still* disabled, apparently, to the satisfaction of whomever reviews my 'case' next time.

Oh, joy. I can't wait.

I wonder if I will need an attorney.

Perhaps the SSA has some reason to believe that new medical technology will be developed during the next 36 months enabling my spine to regenerate itself as the titanium hardware clamped to it mysteriously dissolves and the pain just fades away, like magic, restoring me to my former self at full strength and enabling me to return to a life long since irretrievably lost.

That would be some trick.

I wonder when it was they conveniently removed the word 'permanent' from the dictionary they use.

```
"As you get older three things happen. The
first is your memory goes, and I can't remember
the other two."
 — Sir Norman Wisdom (1915 - 2010), Actor,
Comedian, Singer / Songwriter
```

I will be past normal retirement age if it takes five years to figure it out next time. That fact may render this debate obsolete. Just not for me.

Chapter 09

AUTOMOBILE INSURANCE CLAIM PROCESSING

Lest I forget, I do have a few words about AAA Michigan, the automobile insurance company responsible for paying my accident related medical bills 'for life'.

To give credit where credit is due, this company did pay for both of my surgeries and a fair amount of post-surgical care over the years, in excess of $150,000 in costs if memory serves.

Further, even though I have heard many horror stories regarding insurance claim processing in general in this 'No Fault' state, I identify the company I was insured by at the time of the accidents for accuracy sake and because I prefer to relate my direct experiences rather than rely on hearsay.

I have no reason to doubt that all of the insurance companies are working in collusion with one another to set claims processing policy. I know they share a common claims database. I doubt I would have fared any better simply because the name of the company had been any different. If anyone is to take offense let it be the entire insurance industry. If anyone thinks I am making false accusations let them sue.

Before you begin thinking that $150,000 is a lot of money, try to remember that prior to passage of the No Fault Law, some insurance company would have potentially been on the hook for far more than this, perhaps ten times this amount or more.

The medical bills that get paid by automobile insurance companies now are paid only when they clearly have no choice in the matter since the law requires they do this. My experience says they pay only grudgingly.

The biggest flaw in this system is that it is the insurance company that determines what is accident related and what is not accident related when there should in fact be an impartial third party doing this service. It's kind of like the police policing themselves. It just doesn't work due to the inherent fundamental inequities involved in judging oneself without bias.

My situation is complicated by the fact that I was disabled for most of 2003, 'returned' to work for the next four years but was forced to retire permanently (as a disabled person) in 2008 *as a direct result of the automobile accidents and associated surgeries.*

Automobile insurance policies in Michigan will pay an amount equal to your salary (up to some max amount) if you are declared disabled as a result of a covered vehicular accident and cannot work. They will make these payments for up to 36 consecutive months from the onset of your disability.

If, as I was, you are declared disabled, then 'not' disabled, then disabled again for the same condition, you lose a significant chunk of money you would otherwise have received had you simply remained disabled. When I inquired of AAA Michigan as to the possibility of receiving the two years' worth of lost salary payments I had conveniently skipped they politely informed me that the three year timeframe had long since expired. It was a no go on the $96,000.00

Insufferable Indifference - The Mocking of America

I had missed out on by trying to resume my life when I could have just stopped working instead, but didn't want to.

It is my considered opinion, after careful deliberation, that these funds should be paid out for disabling periods of time related to the same accident even when not consecutive. In other words, I was disabled for three years for the same condition from the same accidents, just not consecutively. I believe anyone in such circumstances should still receive the benefit of these payments to ease their transition into the retired due to disability lifestyle. But no. The insurance companies made sure this cannot happen. At least, mine did.

Not too long after returning to work in 2004 I was required to submit to a medical examination by a doctor of AAA Michigan's choosing or lose all benefits, much like the SSA has done recently.

At least they were decent enough to provide transportation.

During the course of this 'exam' I actually stated to the examining physician that "physical therapy doesn't help me any" and at that point in time this statement was essentially true. The level of pain I was in back then negated any attempt to treat it with physical therapy. Given similar circumstances, if you are as honest a person as I am, you may find yourself wanting to say something stupid like this as well, but I suggest for your own good that you refrain from doing so.

```
"Better to remain silent and be thought a
fool, than to speak and remove all doubt."
 — Abraham Lincoln (1809 - 1865), potentially
paraphrasing Proverbs 17:28; and other persons
in various forms.
```

AAA Michigan subsequently sent me a letter informing me that henceforth they would no longer cover any physical therapy procedures or treatments and, at the time, I did not deem this important or relative to my situation, since this option wasn't helping me anyway.

What I did not find out until years later was that over a long enough period of time the abnormal pain I experience would change character, become slightly less intense and more uniform, such that gentle massage can and does offer some relief from external symptoms and definitely helps to relax the muscles of the shoulders and upper back and so reduce the overall level of discomfort, at least temporarily.

'Massage' is 'physical therapy', something I now need badly and regularly as has been the case for some years now, something that AAA Michigan long ago opted out of paying for simply by sending me a written notice to this effect. Apparently the 'No Fault' law permits a limited amount of time in which to object to changes such as this before it becomes binding upon both parties. You generally have no way to successfully contest changes such as this in any event.

So much for the 'medical coverage for life' theory.

In retrospect it definitely seems possible that someone at AAA Michigan recognized the fact that I was the type of patient who might be a good candidate for lifetime physical therapy treatments, an expensive proposition, and this looked like too good an opportunity to pass up in legally avoiding this particular obligation.

So that is how the automobile insurance companies evade their responsibility to cover payments for your treatments for accident related symptoms. They simply send you to a doctor of their own choosing who, and no real surprise here, more often than not will produce an altogether different evaluation than the one your own medical team recorded. The insurance company can thereafter use this new 'evidence' to deny coverage for 'unrelated' medical procedures.

If you do not object to this within a certain amount of time, and oftentimes even if you do, benefits will be permanently revoked and you are given no recourse to appeal afterwards. Well, you can make a written objection to a state oversight board, as I once did, but if experience is any indication, these people serve only as tools of the insurance companies.

Please keep in mind that before 'No Fault' insurance took effect in Michigan that *someone* would have been responsible for paying my expected missing salary along with an extra penalty for causing all the pain and suffering I have been experiencing for ten straight years now and you can just bet this amount would have been considerable. I believe we are talking in the millions and not the thousands.

None of this is now possible thanks to the 'No Fault' law that, unless I am mistaken, was largely put in place thanks to intensive lobbying efforts on the part of these selfsame insurance companies who wished to eliminate payment of large settlements while at the same time exorbitantly increasing premiums.

They have succeeded admirably in achieving both goals.

They called it 'tort reform' at the time but it would seem to me that the real result of this 'landmark' legislation is that the general population has been reformed out of any kind of bargaining position whatsoever and instead have been assigned a subservient position with no real rights or recourse for mistreatment received at the hands of the all-powerful insurance lobby, the companies that fund them, and their puppets in the state employ, the insurance boards and the legislature.

```
"If you're playing a poker game and you look
around the table and can't tell who the sucker
```

is, it's you."

— Paul Newman (1925 – 2008), Actor, Director, Entrepreneur, Humanitarian...

The bottom line is the insurance company will decide what you need and what you don't need. Period. They will actively seek and will often find any excuse whatsoever to deny a claim or any part of a claim regardless of the actual circumstances. They will do this brazenly and with coldly calculated disregard for your actual circumstances or health. They simply don't care because they don't have to.

The maximum amount the other driver's insurance company will pay as 'damages' under the current No Fault law, if any, according to the attorney representing me at that time, is based on the coverage held by the other driver. This amount can range anywhere from $00,000.00 (uninsured) to $100,000.00, depending on the value specified in their policy, which is based on how much insurance coverage they are willing to pay for.

Again, according to my attorney, this is the maximum you can expect to collect, period, for all damages of any kind resulting from an automobile accident. Right or wrong, this is indeed what happened to me.

Not only this, the other insurance company will try to dicker with you as if at a flea market as to how much of this settlement amount they should actually give you in order to stay out of court. First they will make a very low 'offer'. If it weren't so serious the situation would be laughable. You or your attorney must *negotiate* to collect whatever piddling amount you can get.

"My wife went to the beauty shop and got a

```
mud pack.  For two days she looked nice.  Then
the mud fell off."
```
— Henny Youngman (1906 – 1998), Comedian

While AAA Michigan had no relationship to my employment situation, their doctor found it incumbent upon herself to write up an opinion stating that, among other things apparently, that:

1) I had made the aforementioned statement regarding the ineffectiveness of physical therapy, and that,
2) in her qualified professional opinion there really was nothing wrong with me; I had stopped working voluntarily: I quit working because I wanted to, not because I had to.

This just goes to show the extreme differences of opinion one can receive from so-called qualified professionals, as influenced by who pays the tab.

If you are unfortunate enough to be involved in an automobile accident, be very general with your facts when you fill out the insurance claim form. Be honest, of course, but not too specific.

In my case my credit rating ultimately ended up taking a hit because of what I wrote on the claim form. When I filled it out I apparently wrote that my right shoulder was painful and failed to mention my left shoulder. I was under a lot of stress at the time and wasn't being super careful with my wording, just writing down what I felt at that moment. This would come back to haunt me.

When you have pain in multiple places you generally only feel the one that is the most intense. Other pain seems to fade into the background. In my case, at that time, the right shoulder was the most intense area of extreme discomfort and the left shoulder was unnoticeable.

Also, after two major spinal surgeries on my upper back, each of my shoulders is as bad as the other. They seem to take turns tormenting me.

During the week of Thanksgiving 2009 I experienced what can only be termed as a Major Flare Up. The pain in my left shoulder became so intense I was virtually paralyzed. My entire upper back and neck was on fire. I believe this started on the Tuesday evening before Thanksgiving Day. I tried to do what I usually do, which is to wait it out, but by Wednesday not much had changed.

The pain was somehow reinforcing itself. By the time I realized just how bad this particular episode was going to be it was too late to contact my own doctor who had long since left the office for the upcoming holiday.

I ended up in the local ER seeking the relief that only an injection can provide and, despite a fairly skeptical ER physician who initially thought I might be a drug addict looking for a fix, I did eventually get a small shot providing enough relief to temporarily interrupt the pain cycle.

So how did this experience negatively affect my credit? Here's how:

I just naturally assumed that AAA Michigan would cover the costs of this particular ER visit, no problem. If ever a treatment was related to my accident this was it, given that my usual symptoms had simply been amplified beyond belief. However, this is not what happened.

AAA Michigan spent the next year consistently denying to cover these costs, both hospital and doctor, and here's the kicker: without revealing why. After the time had expired within which I would have had any chance at all of making any kind of appeal I received a letter from them informing me *as a courtesy* that this ER visit was not covered because I had complained about the *wrong* shoulder.

The $1,400.00 payment due the hospital and the $600.00 due the doctor was now my problem. Unfortunately I was unable to cover payment of these bills on my reduced disability income. Now in collection, these issues show up as an 'adverse' item on my credit report and have had a corresponding negative effect on my credit score. Cute.

Oh, did I forget to mention that I lost my house to foreclosure not long after I stopped working? Also in 2009. I was unable to afford the house any longer on my new reduced monthly disability income and had to give it up and get a rental. Such fun.

```
"Men marry women with the hope they will
never change.  Women marry men with the hope
they will change.  Invariably they are both
disappointed."
   — Albert Einstein (1879 - 1955), Physicist
```

Then there was an entirely different episode involving an ambulance company that was unable to file the proper paperwork with AAA Michigan in a timely fashion.

I was at the office of Dr. H for my monthly visit when I began convulsing. I believe this was late 2010 or early 2011. Blame it on a new medicine I had just started taking the week before.

I had received a script for this new med on my previous monthly visit but its fulfillment was delayed for three weeks by AAA Michigan while they determined if it was a covered med, meaning it had to have some relationship to my purported condition; it had to be 'related' to the accident.

The pharmacy mailed it to me when they finally got the go ahead and I began dosing as ordered.

I actually stopped taking this new med after only three days because it made me feel too weird. No doubt the level of this drug in my system was quite low by the time this episode happened but there was apparently still enough to mess me up.

Dr. H called for the emergency medical transport folks when he saw that I was 'unresponsive' and I was summarily whisked away to the local ER where I spent the bulk of the next five hours recovering from this unplanned malady. I don't believe they actually did anything; there really was nothing they could do, so I simply rested 'under observation'.

The doctor eventually concluded I was OK enough to discharge and decided to let me go with instructions to avoid consumption of any more of this new drug. I agreed to comply.

Once released I was stuck at the hospital. My car and phone were back at the doctor's office some miles away. Luckily I had a good friend who agreed to come and give me a lift.

This visit was quite expensive, three times as much as the previous ER visit, but AAA Michigan did eventually pay for it. Except the ambulance company. AAA Michigan claimed they had asked this company for additional documentation 'to substantiate their claim' but didn't receive it so they never paid the $600.00 fee for this service.

Again, by the time I found out anything was seriously wrong, it was long past the time when I could have actually done anything about it, although I do recall telling the ambulance company in writing on more than one occasion to file the proper paperwork if they wished to be paid. This issue is also on my credit report as an 'adverse' item.

```
"The quickest way to double your money is to
```

```
fold it over and put it back in your pocket."
 — Will Rogers (1879 - 1935), Cowboy, Humorist,
Actor
```

So, even though I have an extensive history of 'Paid as Agreed' items going back many, many years, because I have three adverse items on my credit report: one three-and-a-half-year-old foreclosure and two medically inspired insurance related issues, which have been identified as such on the report by means of recording my own note on the item, my score has dropped into the low to mid 600's and the net result is this:

I am considered such a bad credit risk now, even though I've been paying all my other bills on time each month for most of 45 years, that if I wished to borrow $19,000.00 to buy a used car it would cost me $13,000.00 in interest fees.

Neat trick, huh? I'm part of what those in the finance industry affectionately refer as the 'secondary market', or in other words, 'those who can least afford to pay but end up paying the most in interest and fees, and by a wide margin'. I declined this particular transaction when the dealer suggested it.

Chapter 10

OTHER BONES TO PICK

It isn't just the SSA disability processing tedium that concerns me. It isn't just the nightmare they call the Veteran's Administration, which is a subject for another time. I have other bones to pick.

Our society needs more positive reinforcement and less shoot first and ask questions later storm trooper mentality.

I don't know about the rest of you but I grow weary of allowing a privileged few to decide for the rest of us how we should be living our lives. It should be no one's job to be telling me what I should do and what I should not do, what I should look at and what I should not look at; I think I am capable of figuring this out for myself and I believe the vast majority of us are equally capable.

```
"I believe there is something out there watching
us.  Unfortunately, it's the government."
  — Woody Allen (1935 - ), Actor, Writer,
Comedian…
```

None of us needs some other person or group of persons to establish or control what lifestyle choices we can make, either morally or spiritually or any other way you want to think of it. It is none of their business, plain and simple.

Sadly though, we have those among us who actually believe they have to save us from ourselves and damned if they don't go about trying to make this so; failing miserably in the process but unwilling to give up the cause. The Prohibition that was attempted in these United States from 1920 to 1933 is a prime example of such politically oriented suppression of the expression of free choice by the majority.

This experience didn't turn out so well.

More sadly, we did not learn from this experiment, and continue enacting one prohibition after another, also failing miserably but using this very excuse to spend more and more taxpayer dollars in a futile effort to dominate the thoughts and sway the actions of the general population.

Scare tactics are a popular method of influencing public opinion for almost any political purpose, up to and including enactment of the Patriot Act, which, last time I checked, checked the Bill of Rights at the door.

```
"Those who expect to reap the blessings of
freedom must, like men, undergo the fatigue of
supporting it."
 — Thomas Paine (1737 - 1809)
```

The net result of this policy is what we see today: the majority of us serving as slaves of a virtual police state, held hostage by our lifestyle, and not one 'public servant' who wants to be the first to lose their job to downsizing.

A disastrous and irresponsible federal fiscal policy plunging us into so much debt we may never be able to pay it off.

Untold billions of taxpayer dollars going overseas while our own population goes without basic infrastructure maintenance, even as bridges begin collapsing nationwide and sewer systems are overloaded resulting in the wholesale dumping of raw sewage into what should be a pristine environment but is decidedly no longer so.

"Representatives" who have no clue how to represent their constituents or who intentionally ignore same once in office.

```
"Every government degenerates when trusted
to the rulers of the people alone. The people
themselves, therefore, are its only safe
depositories."
 — Thomas Jefferson (1743 - 1826)
 -Notes on the State of Virginia - Query 14,
1781
```

Representative government only works well when those elected actually 'represent' the wishes of the people who elected them instead of the wishes of the special interest groups lining their pockets.

The American people need to take back their government.

We need to reinstate "of the people, by the people and for the people".

We have the technology to permit everyone to vote. Just about everyone has a smart phone now.

Our current system of 'representative' government, while it does employ many positive practices, is two centuries out of date, and also propagates many negative practices.

It is time for a badly needed update.

Here is an example:

```
Should we:
```

a) continue building new courts and prisons to incarcerate thousands of political prisoners; hire and equip large armies of mercenary enforcers and support personnel to persecute and entrap an insignificant but still large portion of the population for essentially victimless crimes to fill these prisons and in so doing self-perpetuate and grow the existing governmental infrastructure.

OR

b) concern ourselves with the industrial pollution that is making our world unlivable?

Press 1 to clean up our act and give our children a habitable planet or Press 9 for more intrusive and suppressive activities by your local and federal authorities who believe they are acting in your best interest and don't really care what you think about it one way or the other or whether you like it or not.

As you can see, phrasing is everything. It is important not only to ask the right questions but to ask them the right way using the right words, else one may inadvertently influence someone's decision. Oops. Advertising 101.

We have technology our forefathers never even dreamed of and we have the intelligence to use these sophisticated tools wisely. We do not have to stick to outdated and antiquated systems devised when there wasn't even any electricity. We can and should change our systems to reflect modern times and abilities while keeping intact the core principles that made our country great:

Life, Liberty and the Pursuit of Happiness Free from Unnecessary Governmental Intrusion into our Daily Lives and Activities!

We don't need to start over but we do need to retune and refine our system of government and we need everyone to join in and help out. We cannot leave this up to our do-nothing gridlocked 'do everything we can to impede the other side while simultaneously accomplishing nothing' elected officials.

We need to ask the hard questions and enforce the hard decisions. This needs to be done responsibly and accurately, yet compassionately. The truth is often obfuscated by idiot beliefs. Discard the idiot beliefs and the truth will be revealed.

```
"We can't solve problems by using the same kind
of thinking we used when we created them."
 — Albert Einstein (1879 - 1955), Physicist
```

We need to put more emphasis on what is really important and de-emphasize that which is not.

For example, putting more emphasis on the study of ways to sway public opinion in an effort to curb violent tendencies and less emphasis on what people choose to do with their own bodies could potentially put a stop to people beating on each other so much.

Global environmental conditions necessitate huge projects in the supporting sciences and in the process would employ millions for the long term. We should investigate this angle.

```
Leaving this planet and colonizing the galaxy
should be a priority.  No, really.
```

Chapter 11

This Phony Drug War and the Morality Police

"The tyranny of a multitude is a multiplied tyranny."
— Edmund Burke (1729 – 1797)
in a letter to Thomas Mercer.

The 'Drug War' is as phony as a four dollar bill. Firstly, you don't wage war against your own people. Secondly and beyond, the end simply does not justify the means.

In reality this homegrown combat is nothing more than an over-inflated politically motivated excuse to employ and equip numerous teams of basically hostile shock troops to be used mainly against the American people and to continuously grow the police / military / homeland security presence.

You have been duped by duplicitous and highly exaggerated propaganda perpetrated by your own not always benevolent government via television, movies and other avenues of advertising.

Make no mistake: the police and court systems are an *industry* devoted to self-perpetuation at any cost and they are making the public pay dearly. This state of affairs is in reality a crime in and of itself of major proportions being perpetrated every day against the so-far unresisting, complacent American public.

What this means is, if there are no actual crimes being committed for prosecution, the ruling elite will find new and inventive ways to create some, basically out of thin air, based on political imperatives, just to keep themselves in business indefinitely, and 'business' means generally screwing over the general public for the maximum amount possible, as often as possible.

```
"The true danger is when liberty is nibbled
away, for expedients, and by parts."
  — Edmund Burke (1729 - 1797)
  - in a Letter to the Sheriffs of Bristol in
1777.
```

It doesn't have to be this way.

Give people hope for the future; give them something to be proud of; give them a good reason to want to get up each morning and cheerfully contribute to the betterment of society; give them these things and you will find that we do not need the parasitic justice system now prevalent in our society or the drugs that have been so vilified.

Careful targeted advertising or what became known as 'yellow journalism' can turn public opinion and often does, even and especially for innocuous activities better left alone.

The best historical example of this dastardly technique is what William Randolph Hearst did in the early 20th century by demonizing marijuana. Because of his reprehensible beliefs and irresponsible actions we have today multiple industries on both sides of the fence, each side employing countless jack-booted commandos killing wantonly while hundreds of billions of dollars change hands annually; all started for no better reason than somebody didn't like it, a very influential somebody, but only one somebody nevertheless.

All of it completely unnecessary and harmful to society in the extreme by taking our attention off of what is really important: our survival as a species.

```
"Liberty must at all hazards be supported.
We have a right to it, derived from our Maker.
But if we had not, our fathers have earned
and bought it for us, at the expense of their
ease, their estates, their pleasure, and their
blood."
  — John Adams (1735 – 1826)
  - A Dissertation on the Canon and Feudal Law,
1765
```

There are many not always obvious reasons behind the passage of laws against the use of drugs that have nothing to do with public safety. Look in your back pocket and you will find very influential medically oriented companies who have a very large stake in the development, production and distribution of all manner of 'substances' and they certainly do not want the public to have easy accessibility to any of their very lucrative products. It is very much in their interests for natural and manufactured 'substances' to be proscribed.

Contrary to what you see on TV and other popular news forums, we don't actually have all that many drug fiends going around robbing and killing everyone who gets in their way. I don't doubt we have some individuals fitting this description running around on occasion, it does happen, but not so many that the rest of us should have any problem making their kind extinct, and not so many that we need millions of hard-drinking, gun-toting belligerent 'law enforcers' who generally go around doing anything they wish because they believe they are exempt from the very laws they allegedly enforce, and sad to say, in many cases, they are exempt.

This is simply not the correct way to approach this issue.

There are at least three major elements to this problem:

Remove the allure of drug use, the mystery and excitement, remove the scandal of it all, the illegality of what is essentially a (ho hum) medical issue in the first place; make drugs readily available to anyone who wants them and you will find that within a generation such people will be a rapidly fading minority by the process of simple elimination.

Remove the need, the desire to escape reality that only desperate poverty can generate. We need to make jobs available to anyone who wants one by creating and funding massive public works projects to maintain or replace our crumbling infrastructure and to prepare for future calamities that are surely coming right around the corner. In case you missed it: all the ice worldwide is melting. This will soon cause major flooding problems for all coastal cities. Perhaps we should give a thought to trying some proactive preservation techniques in place of the 'wait till it happens, then react' philosophy so commonly used today.

Dismantle the 'justice industry', remove the profit motive, and watch the 'drug problem' fade away like some kind of bad memory.

```
"I am for doing good to the poor, but I differ
in opinion of the means. I think the best way
of doing good to the poor, is not making them
```

easy in poverty, but leading or driving them out of it. In my youth I travelled much, and I observed in different countries, that the more public provisions were made for the poor, the less they provided for themselves, and of course became poorer. And on the contrary, the less was done for them, the more they did for themselves, and became richer."
— Ben Franklin (1706 - 1790), in 1766

These so-called enforcers of law and order go about their business equipped with the latest and greatest hardware acquired using your dime. This may or may not turn out good for you. It didn't for me.

Here is my personal experience from the nineties:

No one was at home one fine sunshiny workday afternoon when my house was entered into by police representing the township of West Bloomfield, Michigan. They simply climbed through an open window in my son's room and began searching the house without first obtaining a valid search warrant.

"One of the most essential branches of English liberty is the freedom of one's house. A man's house is his castle."
— James Otis (1725 - 1783), in 1761

The responding officers justified their actions using the case law doctrine known as 'exigent circumstances' based on a reported sighting of two teens loitering at the window. 'Exigent circumstances' is supposed to mean they are in hot pursuit of a known felon or they have reason to believe a crime is currently being committed on the premises.

Amendment IV to the United States Constitution:
The right of the people to be secure in their persons, houses, papers, and effects, against unreasonable searches and seizures, shall not be violated, and no Warrants shall issue, but upon probable cause, supported by Oath or affirmation, and particularly describing the place to be searched, and the persons or things to be seized.

Claiming this circumstance gives the police legal authority to enter any premises without a search warrant for the purpose of conducting an impromptu search in violation of the fourth amendment to the U.S. constitution.

If, while looking for the alleged criminal activities, anything of an 'illegal' nature is observed just by happenstance; say, a few grains of white powder in the carpet in the closet under a pile of boxes and clothing, which would seem to be the last place a burglar would hide, why then this is fair game for prosecution of the occupants.

According to the witness who had observed the entire incident from start to finish and subsequently reported same to the police, the two teens had left the premises *without* entering the house, and the responding officers were informed of this fact before anything else happened.

These champions of justice were not satisfied.

They drew their weapons and went into the house to root out the evil they believed was lurking within, to make sure my family and I would be safe from these dangerous teenage psychopathic killer intruders once we came home.

At least, this is the way the prosecutor later explained their actions.

```
"They that can give up essential liberty to
purchase a little temporary safety, deserve
```

neither liberty nor safety."
— Ben Franklin (1706 - 1790), in 1759

Moreover, any discovery of any kind of any allegedly illegal material observed upon entry into the premises apparently gives the police license to search the entire home from top to bottom with a fine tooth comb, no matter how many hours it may take or how many evidence technicians need to be called in to do the job thoroughly and completely.

What really happened is the police took advantage of this alleged burglary report to 'legally' enter and search my house without the bothersome necessity of securing a proper search warrant beforehand, something they would not have been able to secure in any event due to the lack of any evidence in support of this procedure.

The police intruders looked for the alleged criminal intruders in every nook and cranny, every room, every closet, every cabinet and every drawer. They searched high and low leaving no sock unturned. Keep in mind that anything found in the course of conducting their search that may be of an apparent illegal nature, even if unrelated to their original purpose for entering the house, will be confiscated and prosecuted to the full extent of the law.

There was nothing in the house for them to find but this did not stop them from trying their very best to find it anyway. They even looked for the intruders inside the wife's jewelry box.

According to one neighbor, they remained in my house conducting their exhaustive search for at least four hours, despite being denied a search warrant, which warrant was requested *after* they had already entered the house and began their exhaustive search.

```
"But a Constitution of Government once changed
from Freedom, can never be restored. Liberty
once lost is lost forever."
   — John Adams (1735 - 1826), letter to Abigail
Adams, 1775
```

These police searched every square inch of the house, going through every room with a fine tooth comb and even later cheerfully admitted to this activity when I inquired of the officer who stopped by my home one afternoon to ask if he could search my son's room again. He also took this opportunity to very seriously inform me that I too would have been prosecuted had anything been found anywhere else in the house during that fateful first search, this being the very officer who had instigated same. He was concerned that I was harboring a drug addict and wanted to help out with his 'recovery'.

During their impromptu search they found and collected microscopic amounts of some substance from the carpeting of my son's closet which had been concealed underneath a pile of clothing, 'evidence' that was consumed by laboratory testing leaving nothing for the defense, along with some kind of so-called 'drug paraphernalia'. I think it was a bong.

Apparently the police, or at least this one particular officer, had been tipped that my son was a major drug dealer (not). I didn't find this out until I connected the dots afterwards but this overzealous officer had long been seeking an opportunity to search my house. When the so-called burglary report came in he jumped all over it. For all I know it was he who arranged for the two teenagers to be seen at the window. I'm not ruling out anything.

The brazen effrontery exhibited by the officer behind this search in a country where the populace is supposed to be protected from illegal search and seizure by the constitution should send a chill down your spine. It did mine and still does. What is worse still is that he got away with it scot-free.

He was subjected to no repercussions that I am aware of for breaking into and searching my house without first securing a valid warrant. On the contrary, he may have been rewarded.

```
"Nothing in the world is more dangerous than
sincere ignorance and conscientious stupidity."
— Dr. Martin Luther King, Jr. (1929 - 1968)
```

I arrived home from work and discovered the damaged screen (window now closed). It looked like someone had broken into the house. Someone had. They were wearing police uniforms.

Around 9 p.m. that evening the same two officers who had conducted this unwarranted and highly questionable search earlier along with their fellow deputies (evidence technicians) showed up at the front door expressing mock concern regarding any suspicious activity I may have noticed at the house that day.

I stated that it looked as if there had been a break-in.

"Oh, that was us" says one of the officers, smiling at me with his best confident look. The other officer actually looked uncomfortable, almost apologetic.

The real reason they had come to the house was to confirm that the room where they had found the microscopic 'evidence' was in fact occupied by my son.

Now, you would think any court in the land would reject this illegally confiscated evidence, yes? It happens that way on TV every day, creating no end to the problems experienced by today's celebrity champions of law and order.

Guess again.

The next few years were made a living hell for both my son and myself by both the police and the courts of the region. The cost for me ran into the tens of thousands of dollars. I was barely able to keep my son out of prison. He was forced to pee in a bottle (daily) with a caustic observer standing nearby leering and laughing. This was *not* a medical setting. To add insult to injury we had to pay for this particular activity on a per-pee basis.

```
"To compel a man to furnish funds for the
propagation of ideas he disbelieves and abhors
is sinful and tyrannical."
  — Thomas Jefferson (1743 - 1826)
  - Virginia Statutes of Religious Freedom,
1779
```

You have to ask yourself: what kind person would want a job watching other people pee? How exactly would that job interview go? What kind of perverted system would even offer such an employment opportunity? I can tell you. It is the oppressive system of justice we now have hovering over us like Damocles' sword.

Where but in an Orwellian society does the ruling authority feel it incumbent upon themselves to minutely monitor the bodily fluids of the populace?

```
"When bad men combine, the good must associate;
else they will fall one by one, an unpitied
sacrifice in a contemptible struggle."
  — Edmund Burke (1729 - 1797)
  Thoughts on the Cause of Present Discontent
- 1770
```

Add to this the constant harassment doled out by the local police as they conducted impromptu vehicle searches of my son's car on a regular basis without ever finding what they were looking for. This happened at least a dozen times, before and after the house search.

Talk about a nightmare. This was definitely one of those.

I was forced to sell the house and move to another town just to get any peace and quiet. All because of one overzealous jerk in the West Bloomfield Township police department who thought the drug war was his own private fiefdom, that his mission in life and his job entitled him to abusively seek and destroy all miscreants. Particularly those miscreants attending the local high school. If nothing else they make easy targets.

The entire affair was contrived. None of it needed to happen. My son had been doing some harmless experimenting, that's all. Who among us has not done this at least once?

The scuttlebutt I eventually got from the very expensive attorney I was forced to hire to represent my son against this nefarious attack by the ruling establishment was that it was very lucky for me that he was found to be a casual user because as a result of this, and only because of this, my house would not be confiscated. Lucky me.

The ultimate sadness to me is that so many sacrificed so much for so little.

Many, many tens of thousands of people have laid their lives on the line and a far greater number have been maimed so that we can (in theory) enjoy constitutional protection from abusive police and governmental intervention specifically directed at controlling, removing or disregarding our personal liberties and activities.

The fact that some individuals / groups are abusing the legislative system, and worse still, will sidestep this process and use the bureaucratic system instead, to enact ever stricter controls over our day to day lives, to trick us using scare tactics or to compel us using military type force or to fool us by manipulating the media into some particular behavior or way of thinking based on any political (or religious) agenda, this makes a complete mockery of the sacrifice made by all the people who voluntarily gave up their lives or health to guarantee our freedom to speak and act freely without fear of retribution.

It is with the greatest of sorrow when I realize the ultimate sacrifice made by these Great Champions is made meaningless by the pedantic thinking of so-called lawmakers nationwide and their efforts to control and regulate every aspect of our lives when in fact this is not necessary. Unless one is in an actual active duty military situation, one is not the property of the government and one does not need unsolicited guidance or direction for personal functioning from same.

Complacency on the part of the general population has led to a situation wherein so-called authority can conveniently disregard constitutional protections whenever the need arises. Worse still, they are getting away with it, as if this behavior is perfectly acceptable because the end results merit it.

To have our constitutionally guaranteed rights systematically stripped from us without even a by your leave, not by a foreign power, but by the very people who are supposed to be safeguarding them, in the guise of promoting safety or national security, is particularly disturbing to me and it should be to you as well.

We need to put more focus on the reasons why someone chooses to abuse any substance and less focus on the actual usage which should actually be a medical issue and not a legal issue.

We need to continually rethink and re-examine our moral imperatives in light of new developments.

Give people hope for the future, provide meaningful jobs and a clean environment to live in, and any desire for the overuse of artificial depressants and stimulants will mostly disappear. The *abuse*, not the use. *Use* is a medical issue, *abuse* may become a legal issue, depending on circumstances, and is certainly to be avoided by anyone with half a noggin.

Maintaining *criminal* records and locking up a significant minority of people for years in huge new prisons because they choose to smoke marijuana, not only is this not a priority, it should be classified as an abuse of power and any such official activity as this should be stopped immediately.

Furthermore, those already incarcerated for nothing more than possession should be released and their 'criminal' records purged.

```
"One has a moral responsibility to disobey
unjust laws."
    — Dr. Martin Luther King, Jr. (1929 - 1968)
```

Making criminals out of people who don't deserve it is a big part of the problem we need to solve. I don't know about you but I can't afford such prisons. My tax dollars would be better spent on other more beneficial activities such as fixing all the broken bridges existing on the nation's highways, just for starters.

There is no such thing as a marijuana 'addict' because tetrahydrocannabinol (THC) has no addictive properties beyond those some people afflict themselves with voluntarily. Marijuana imbibers are by and large very mellow relaxed folks posing a threat to no one. If no smoke is handy it really is no big deal. It can wait. No doubt about it. I *know* because I've been there, done that.

I know wherefrom I speak having had many years of actual

experience with this particular subject matter as a Medical Marijuana consumer.

Before you go Leaping to Inaccurate Conclusions consider this: only someone who has taken (legal) morphine (meaning insurance will cover this cost) over an extended period of time (many years) can truly appreciate the advantages of (potentially 'illegal') Medical Marijuana (meaning insurance companies do not cover the cost) for relief above and beyond what is offered by the prescription medication and with virtually no systemic side effects.

Despite the (undeserved) societal prohibitions regarding marijuana usage, I will take this product any day over morphine or any other so-called 'pain' medication currently on the market whether derived from opiates or otherwise and not just because I am allergic to most of them, and not because I'm just some misguided doper, a Dude if you will, looking to be perpetually stoned.

The effectiveness of the properties of this non-addictive 'substance' THC in alleviating the symptoms of persistent pain or even chronic pain is something I can testify to personally. It helps. Period. And without all the side effects so prevalent in modern 'pain relieving' prescription substances the medical establishment favors over this not so simple herb.

As regarding more severe drugs, excluding alcohol, if any one individual chooses to escape reality in this fashion, give them the proper and necessary warnings so they will know what to expect. Then, assuming they have made the necessary funeral arrangements, if they still decide to pursue this avenue of inquiry, let 'em have at it; the quicker the better and without harming anyone else. The sooner we weed these people out of the gene stock the better.

The cost to society would be cheaper by orders of magnitude.

We also would no longer need a large army of people with sadistic tendencies using the issue of drug use as an excuse to legally abuse a small but not insignificant segment of the population numbering in the millions.

Again, this is a medical issue, not a legal issue. Legal issues arise from those who abuse or misuse, not those who use.

Oh, I have no doubt the 'authorities' will dispute such a position.

This particular issue serves to finance quite a bit of their operations. Change would be undesirable for those in a position of power over others. They might lose their (unnecessary) job. Better to maintain the status quo than to do anything that might actually be sensible.

These people hide behind their badges, their weapons, their bullet proof glass and their indifferent attitude, pretending, to themselves mostly, that they are defenders of law and order, that they are actually helping society. The real truth is that most of them are cowardly bullies taking sadistic pleasure in f'ng with other people.

The costume they wear; sorry, *uniform*, and all the trappings of office leads many incumbents to believe they can do whatever they please whenever they please. Some actually delude themselves into believing they are doing the right thing. One cardinal rule they seem to operate by is that since they enforce the law, they are above the law, and not subject to the punishments they dole out to everyone else.

I think we will find on closer examination that the system is bloated beyond belief and no one wants to lose their job to downsizing. The only way to perpetuate and grow such a system, and you better believe this is their intent, is to go out and find people to charge with 'crimes'. As many crimes as possible. The more the merrier. If that means setting up a sting operation then so be it.

We all know how dangerous prostitutes and the men looking for a little unattached sex can be, yes? They generally have a lot of money and they can pay big fines. This is why it is illegal (except in Nevada and Amsterdam). Not because they are such dangerous individuals, not because they are a major threat to society or in fact even bothering anyone except some lonely wife somewhere, but because they can pay and pay generously.

```
"The big difference between sex for money
and sex for free is that sex for money usually
costs a lot less."
 - Brendan Behan (1923 - 1964), Poet, Writer
```

Alcohol falls into a category of its own and in many respects is far more dangerous than drug use has ever been or will ever be. Drug users by and large only wish to be left alone to indulge; they seek anonymity, they wish to remain in the background and so unnoticed; they do not ordinarily go out of their way looking for trouble or drawing attention to themselves.

Alcohol, on the other hand, can and does incite violent tendencies that would under normal nonalcoholic circumstances be dormant or nonexistent. I am fairly sure this fact is indisputable. People high on alcohol can be very aggressive and abusive, period. Not all people of course, but enough to create a problem. If these people end up in prison, it is not because they drink, but because of what happens when they drink.

Drinking in and of itself is not illegal. It's what you do immediately afterwards that may cause problems. Driving is a real bad idea! The same should hold true for drug use. It should not be the use of, but only the resulting consequences of the abuse of, if any, that one should be held accountable for.

The Drug War has been and still is being used as an overinflated excuse to militarize the nation's police and to systematically subjugate and steal from the people. The 'system' does not serve to protect the people, it serves to protect the system. The logo 'To Serve and Protect' refers not to any service provided for the people who are coerced into paying all the bills; instead this phrase refers to what the police do for the ruling political elite and for themselves. Kind of like pouring salt into your wound and then enjoying your reaction, even laughing. This is what they do. With relish.

It is only by rising up in unison that we can cast off the societal shackles placed upon us by previous generations whose sense of justice was rooted in the wood shed mentality.

It is only by working together as a cohesive group, as organized government is doing in its attempt to orchestrate our behavior, that we can really have any chance at all to protect ourselves and our families from such abuse as is now prevalent.

It is only by reexamining the reasons behind each law in the light of reason that we can truly determine the necessity of letting it remain on the books as an effective instrument of humanistic justice.

Maximum creativity is concomitant with maximum freedom.

We can be stifled or we can be free. The choice is ours to make: status quo or bold new future. It is up to us, the population at large, 'the people', to recognize such politically abusive behavior for what it is and, furthermore, to put a stop to it. Peacefully, if at all possible. I do not advocate violence but sometimes we do not get to make that choice, it gets made for us.

Sadly, we have to keep in mind that many of those in a position of power in this country will resist any change not in keeping with their own interests; they will not voluntarily relinquish their control. These are violently oriented people. Why else would they choose an occupation that lets them carry weapons and gives them dominance over the bulk of the population? The *like* to inflict pain. This is how they get their kicks.

Why else would they cleverly protect themselves from any reprisals by hiding behind bullet proof glass and metal detectors; their weapons and military tactics their shield? It is because they *know* that what they are doing is wrong. This is why they fear reprisal from the general population. Anyone who thinks such folks as this will peacefully accept any changes jeopardizing their way of life may be in for a nasty surprise.

I do not have any magic bullets to fix these issues aside from recommending we give people hope for the future by enacting massive public works projects which would also invigorate private enterprise *and* simultaneously make government at all levels smaller and less intrusive in our everyday lives. The future our children will face will be bleak indeed if we do not soon take action to correct the inequities currently prevalent in our society.

```
"I have yet to see any problem, however
complicated, which, when you looked at it
in the right way, did not become still more
complicated".
— Poul Anderson (1926 - 2001), Writer
```

People died so we could be free. A *lot* of people. This is a debt that can only be paid by preserving the main reason for which they made this sacrifice: the enjoyment of personal liberty free from unwarranted intrusion by 'authority'.

Can we be so callous as to disrespect their memory by allowing the picayune mind to prevail?

Can we really afford to be so complacent as to hand our children a society riddled with puritanical platitudes?

The only thing I can really say for sure is that the longer this situation goes on the harder it will be to fix it.

Chapter 12

MISSYGIRL THE CALICO CAT

There may be those among you who are wondering why there are excerpts from *Missygirl the Calico Cat* in this book.

The reason is simple.

I wish to draw your attention to her series of books.

I began writing these children's books for three very good reasons.

One, this activity, writing, which I can only do part time each day, is helping me to keep my sanity, or at least I hope so. Being creative again delivers its own reward as well.

Two, if I can entertain and educate children at the same time, perhaps some good will be done.

Three, and most importantly, I want to be able to donate large sums to children's hospitals to honor my Mom and I want to be able to donate equally large sums to animal rescue organizations to honor my Dad.

But…

I don't have nearly as much money as I would like to give to these worthy causes.

So…

If I can get folks to buy my children's story books then I can give all the royalties to deserving organizations whose philosophy matches my own: little or no overhead, everything goes to the needy. And, as an added bonus, folks get something they can read and enjoy for years to come.

Everyone wins!

So there it is, all laid out plain and simple.

My new job is to write and publish these books for as long as I am capable of doing so. And to set up a foundation to handle affairs in my absence to make sure the funds go to the right places in perpetuity.

'The right places' would be only those organizations falling into one of the categories mentioned above: those that do the most good, that have little or no overhead, that give everything to the needy without seeking personal gain in the process.

Your new job is to get your copies of these fantastic new reasonably priced children's books, available as individual paperback or in eBook format, to read, enjoy and treasure as a new classic!

All currently available editions can be easily found by searching the World Wide Web for *Missygirl the Calico Cat*.

I am quite confident that by working together we can make a positive difference in the quality of life for many, many individuals.

The Missygirl the Calico Cat Charitable Foundation, coming soon to a tax advantaged state near you, hopes you will join in.

Enjoy the entertaining stories and sleep good knowing that you have helped out some very worthy causes!

Chapter 13
OFFICIALDOM GONE CRAZY

There is a thirty-six square mile postage stamp on the face of the earth located in southeast Michigan officially known as the Charter Township of Commerce that is affectionately referred to as Commerce Charter Township by those in the area who dislike using the word 'of'.

As far as I know this is the only place on earth where Commerce Road going east/west meets Commerce Road going north/south. This might not seem so strange except it happens in more than one place. Further, there are several businesses in the area who claim to have an address on East West Maple Road. Truly. This even makes a kind of sense if you think about it long enough.

If that doesn't give you some idea of how the people in this area think I'm not sure what will but I'm going to give it my best shot anyway because I promised I would expose them as the pompous, anal, stuffed-shirt fools that I believe them to be. I'm quite sure they hope I will say something stupid so I can be held liable for libel.

Let's find out, shall we?

This former resort area, dotted with small lakes and swamps, sports a landscape with some rolling hills and many sections of farmland, much of which has now been suburbanized.

There are large areas of swampland, affectionately referred to as wetlands, all filled up with cattails and all manner of wildlife: birds, deer, skunks, squirrels, opossum, chipmunks, etc., which, sadly, can be seen as abundant road kill on all the area roads.

There is a great deal of secondary forest, meaning there are an awful lot of trees. Tens of thousands of trees would be putting it lightly. Millions, even, but who's counting?

Attend me as I regale you with the bizarre mocking events that occurred in this place to someone near and dear to my heart as I was finishing this book.

It is only because of the extreme strangeness of these events, my extreme distaste at their inanity and the fact that this is a prime example of Insufferable Indifference and The Mocking of America, that I was inspired to include these facts here.

These events are so strange they will stretch your credulity to the breaking point but I can assure you that everything I am about to tell you is the truth, the whole truth and nothing but. So help me.

There is within the township a place known as Dodge Park V, a place with walking trails, ball fields and small forested areas, and this is where the wife was walking with her dog Daisy (a Sheltie) one fine sunny afternoon when she stumbled on a situation whereupon one tree had fallen upon another and in so doing had disrooted and damaged the unfortunate three foot spruce sapling on the bottom.

Now, most of us would hardly have even noticed this happenstance and would have kept walking. Trees come and trees go and the vast majority of us don't really notice one way or another. But, my wife is a member of a decidedly small club consisting of a select few who actually feel empathy for all manner of living things, both plant and animal, an empathy so strong it compels action when confronted with a circumstance such as this. This little twig, which for all intents and purposes was a goner in any event, no more than a small branch really, called out to her and she decided she had no choice but to try to help it survive.

```
"The love for all living creatures is the
most noble attribute of man."
 — Charles Darwin (1809 - 1882)
```

In broad daylight, in full view of hundreds of other people in the park, in the midst of uncountable trees of all sizes, with only the best of intentions and not trying to hide anything, this elderly lady tenderly took up this small damaged sapling and took it with her, placing it in the backseat of the car she was driving so she could properly tend to it at a more propitious moment.

Then it occurred to her that a bit of the native soil just might give this little tree a better chance at survival and off she went with a small garden shovel that just happened to be in the trunk and a small plastic bag, taken off a roll we keep in the car, to retrieve a small amount of this soil from the forest. I believe the presence of this shovel was coincidental and there never was any actual premeditation to gather plants nor was there any deliberate intent on her part to violate any laws.

It wasn't long after this that she is confronted by one officer (name removed) demanding to know what she is doing.

```
"Property is theft. Nobody 'owns' anything.
When you die, it all stays here."
 — George Carlin (1937 - 2008), Comedian
```

Now, stay with me here and try to picture a five foot, elderly, reasonably frail little old lady from eastern Europe with a limited command of the English language walking in the woods with her small dog, basically minding her own business and doing no real harm, who is terrified of any police authority in the first place and for good reason, having not had many favorable experiences with same, being confronted by a much larger uniformed, armed, basically unfriendly and sneeringly disrespectful person *who has actually been searching the woods for her* along with another stout representative of the law, only of the female persuasion, who hasn't yet happened upon this scene.

```
"To argue with a man who has renounced
the use and authority of reason, and whose
philosophy consists in holding humanity in
contempt, is like administering medicine to
the dead, or endeavoring to convert an atheist
by scripture."
  — Thomas Paine (1737 - 1809),
```
The American Crisis

Her crime?

In her bid to save this little twig which she had found lying on the ground being crushed by a much larger tree, in the midst of thousands upon tens of thousands of other secondary growth trees, she had had the audacity to remove this small twig from the forest and put it in her car.

Two police cruisers were dispatched to apprehend the potentially dangerous, now clearly confused little old lady walking with her dog in the woods and reportedly harvesting trees wholesale.

In an odd twist of fate, but mainly owing to differences in interpretation, what she viewed as a rescue operation they viewed as a theft. She was clearly trying to make off with the tiny sapling.

An audacious crime in broad daylight! The very nerve! This called for swift justice!

So it was that officer (name removed), blithely ignoring anything my wife had to say about just trying to help out, who is now joined by some other officer serving as backup no doubt in case the little old lady should attack, forcibly confiscates said twig from the car while simultaneously extracting a full confession from one very confused trembling little old lady.

He summarily issues a citation for *larceny* in the park, a misdemeanor and a violation of a *local ordinance* to wit: taking twig, for which the penalty can be 93 days in jail and a $500 fine plus legal fees plus court costs. Have a nice day!

```
"A general dissolution of principles and
manners will more surely overthrow the liberties
of America than the whole force of the common
enemy. While the people are virtuous they cannot
be subdued; but when once they lose their virtue
then will be ready to surrender their liberties
to the first external or internal invader."
— Samuel Adams (1722 - 1803), in 1779
```

Now, I don't know about you, but where I come from this is considered overkill in the extreme.

Instead of exhibiting even the littlest bit of common sense or respect for this dignified elderly lady, instead of just politely explaining to this obviously confused dowager that she must leave the forest foliage undisturbed, instead of accepting her simple explanation and taking five minutes to just replant the little sapling then and there, instead of acting the least bit reasonably, these champions of justice roll all over her and frighten her to no end.

Apparently they considered their behavior justified using the 'just doing my job' mentality, perhaps based on some ill-defined job description regarding the proper procedure for hassling little old ladies walking with dog in park picking up twigs, most likely required training based on the severity involved. She thought she got a ticket. She wasn't sure why.

What she got was slammed. Hard! But didn't know it.

When a little old lady walking her dog in the park becomes the target of a police dragnet because she tries to rescue a single solitary twig then we know we officially have Officialdom Gone Crazy.

```
"Two things are infinite: the universe and
human stupidity; and I'm not sure about the
universe."
    — Albert Einstein (1879 - 1955), Physicist
```

The police here must be exceedingly bored or the township is very hard up for money, or both, to be conducting this kind of impromptu search operation. I can only imagine how many times hordes of horticultural hobbyists clear-cut the local groves of trees on the sly before township officials realized the need for enacting such a restrictive ordinance as they obviously have in place now.

I took it upon myself to contact the township board of trustees in an effort to see if they would voluntarily withdraw the ridiculous charges that had been filed. Here is the letter I mailed to them verbatim with alterations to protect the innocent and / or because I cannot justify identifying these people by name; mainly because it seems to me that it makes little difference what name they go by, the result would surely be the same. And yes, my letter is not entirely polite.

TO: Board of Trustees, Commerce Township   8 May 2013
Supervisor   *Treasurer*
Name 1   Name 2

Trustee   *Trustee*   *Trustee*   *Trustee*
Name 3   Name 4   Name 5   Name 6

2009 Township Drive
Commerce Township, Michigan 48390

RE: Citation 130Snnnnn issued dd mmm @ hh:mm

Sir or Madam:

Frankly, I am stunned.

My 63-year-old wife is out walking her dog at Dodge Park 5 on a sunny Friday afternoon when she comes across a spruce sapling being crushed by a larger tree that has fallen on it.

(My wife) is a good hearted person. She felt bad for this little tree and decided to rescue it.

With only the best of intentions, without trying to hide anything, in full view of hundreds of other people at the park, she took this little tree and put it in the back seat of our car.

Next thing you know she is surrounded by police cars. She tries to explain to two very unfriendly individuals that she is only trying to be helpful but the disrespectful officers refuse to listen to anything she has to say. Instead, (officer name removed) decides to issue this insane ticket.

My wife was trying to save a tree. She meant no harm. But a walk in the park became a walk into hell. I have to take her to the 52nd district court to be arraigned for this heinous crime. I have to come up with between $1,500 and $6,000 to hire an attorney to keep her out of jail and pay court costs. Lovely!

I am disabled and on a fixed income. I am a veteran. The two are not related. My wife is a (country removed) immigrant who does not necessarily understand all of our customs. She did what she did innocently.

I honestly have to wonder what caliber of person would do such a thing as this. I have to wonder what kind of police officer could be such a blithering idiot. I have to wonder what kind of township would support these activities.

You people make me sick. You should be ashamed of yourselves, each and every one of you, but especially (officer name removed).

Sincerely,

Yours Truly

cc
Editor, Detroit Free Press, 615 W. Lafayette Blvd, Detroit, MI 48226
Listings Editor, Metro Times, 733 St. Antoine, Detroit, MI 48226
(Popular Talk Show Host) Peter Werbe, c/o WRIF, 1 Radio Plaza, Ferndale, MI 48220

These dedicated individuals, instead of throwing out these exceedingly stupid charges, decide instead to ignore me completely, as expected, apparently agreeing that prosecution is justified. Can't have little old ladies going around harvesting the local forest! Next thing you know she will come in the dark of night with a backhoe to do some real damage!

I imagine they were only following the advice of legal counsel not to actually communicate with anyone living in the area who may be negatively impacted by their narrow-minded behavior but somehow this doesn't make me feel any better.

So it was I shelled out $1,500.00 for an attorney to represent her at a pretrial hearing at the 52-1 district courthouse in Novi one day in May.

```
"Good people do not need laws to tell them
to act responsibly, while bad people will find
a way around the laws."
 — Plato (427-347 B.C.)
```

There is at this particular courthouse one whacky judge I am personally aware of who believes he is a king; that his courtroom is his own private fiefdom and that all should bow in obeisance to his holiness. I am not exaggerating in the slightest bit when I tell you I saw firsthand his outrageous behavior as he endlessly baited then berated a (substance abusing) dreadlocked teen appearing before him as the parents stood nearby watching helplessly, unable to say or do anything or risk being held in contempt themselves.

I think I was in the courtroom to consummate the dreaded equipment violation repair confirmation sequence. The only contemptible thing I saw was this judge performing his improv for his own amusement.

He was practically salivating as he ordered his aid to remove the miscreant from the courtroom and take hair samples to be analyzed for consumption of banned substances, and should anything be found, woe be it unto this imperfect excuse for a human being.

I will not justify this judge's existence by naming him but anyone who has been there knows who I mean.

Appearing before this particular judge could potentially turn this shindig my wife was in into a real nightmare.

Luckily, we did not see the aforementioned lunatic, but instead drew Judge P., who apparently has more common sense than everyone else in the town put together. As a bit of a naturalist himself, he understood what it was my wife was trying to do that day in the park; he understood that she had simply taken what to her were only innocent actions which could have been easily explained and remedied instead of being turned into the circus it had become.

Even so, his hands were tied by procedure.

Judge P. did what he could to set the record straight, which consisted of throwing out the larceny charge and substituting a disorderly charge. He took the matter *under advisement,* which is court talk for: 'promise to be good and it will all disappear in thirty days', as if it never happened. Court costs: $325.00.

Again, he had no choice.

An afternoon walk in the park turned into an afternoon walk into hell, costing me $1,825.00 out of pocket all at once, not counting time, travel and overall aggravation. This is a tidy sum for a disabled veteran (unrelated) on a fixed income to have to pay because someone else was having a bad day. I really don't appreciate these people reaching into my pocket and taking this money. They didn't actually deserve it and I didn't actually have it to give.

As far as I am concerned a theft did occur here but it is nothing my wife did.

The actions taken by the local yokel reporting this heinous crime and by the (unresponsive) responding police could have and should have been avoided as unnecessary or amended by the simple expedient of using common courtesy and respect when interacting with the public, something they are supposed to be trained to do.

If these people truly have nothing better to do than to go out of their way to hassle little old ladies walking in the park then they are seriously in need of some motivational adjustments as to what constitutes a real crime.

I heartily recommend you give Commerce Charter Township a pass due to the high level of Insufferable Indifference for the use of common sense and an almost complete lack of respect for individual liberties that is to be found here.

Chapter 14

SELF-EVIDENT TRUTHS

It is not always easy to know when something is right but it is generally very obvious when something is wrong. Folks, I'm here to tell ya, we have a problem, more than one actually, and the longer we ignore it (them) the worse off everyone is going to be when the s—t really hits the fan, which it will eventually do.

Our current level of technology permits the recording of pretty much every digital interchange that occurs. Everything. This data can then be subjected to intelligent analysis by anyone possessing the appropriate computer system. Big Brother is for real now. George Orwell got it right.

People with small minds paying bullies with no minds are running the show. The money they are using is yours, impounded by means of exorbitant compulsory taxation or outright confiscation. This situation is not going to change as long as these sorts of people are focused on and capable of enriching themselves and their cohorts at your expense.

Some taxation is necessary to provide for the common good: essential services, defense, transportation network, etc. Anything beyond this; any funds seized by any governmental entity for any reason whatsoever which is then used in any attempt to control how the people think or monitor what the people do in the privacy of their own homes, this must be stopped. It simply is none of their (official) beez wax, period.

It should be no one's business to be telling me my business. Exceptions to this rule? Perhaps under some medically induced circumstances. Perhaps if one's egregious personal behavior offends society in an unacceptable fashion of one sort or another and intervention is not only warranted but unavoidable.

The purpose of government is not in devising nefarious means of surreptitiously controlling the way people behave or in directing the actions of the populace; it is rather the other way around, although we seem to have lost track of this idea somewhere along the line.

The interests of governmental propagation and the interests of individual personal freedoms are just naturally opposed to one another.

The time has come to set aright what has been allowed to go astray: the security of the individual to be free from unwarranted governmental intrusion.

Machines operate by codified rule sets. People do not. And should not have to.

How we go about doing this is not for me to decide although I can offer some suggestions.

Any such list as this is necessarily incomplete and subject to revision or addition, but only for good reasons. Let me see if I can get us started in the right direction.

In addition to the original Constitution of the United States of America and the attendant Bill of Rights, which laws should be honored and observed and not negated by subsequent 'case law', we should hold these truths to be self-evident and in no particular order:

- Government exists to serve the people and not the other way around.
- The civil rights of the individual shall not be denied, abridged or otherwise encumbered for any reason whatsoever excepting armed conflict.
- Religion and politics *must* be kept separate.
- The innate dignity of each person should be recognized and respected.
- Individual liberties should not be discarded in the name of safety or security.
- The greatest benefit to society is achieved by permitting maximum personal freedoms to each individual.
- The ability for self-expression shall not be limited or otherwise restricted by any moral dogma.
- Belief systems come and go and each person should be allowed to choose their own free from coercion.
- The curious mind should be rewarded with access to information instead of being shut down by stifling doctrine.
- Each individual should have the chance to advance according to their own abilities.
- Each person has something to contribute and they should be allowed to do so.
- People have the right to be and to do whatever they wish as long as not directly causing harm to another.
- The right of the individual to be free in their personal pursuits trumps the right of the government to enact oppressive behavioral strictures based on moral imperatives.
- Our best chance for success is based on trust, respect and cooperation amongst all people.
- The majority may rule but this does not grant intelligence to

same.
- The minority will rule the majority by any means necessary, including deadly force, as long as they are permitted to do so.
- The right of the people to rise up and cast off the shackles placed on them by oppressive government policies shall not be denied.
- We should not be held hostage by small-minded people seeking to perpetuate the status quo against all reason.
- Citizen's homes and possessions are exempt from civil intrusion without a proper warrant signed by three qualified magistrates. No exceptions.
- Free people are capable of arriving at the right conclusion on their own without being told what to think or what to do by targeted advertisements paid for using tax dollars.
- Psychological warfare is an ongoing project at all levels of government aimed at the citizenry in an effort to sway opinion towards the prevailing political position. If this cannot be stopped it must be counter-balanced with the presentation of opposing viewpoints so people have the chance to decide for themselves using all the facts.
- The time to act is now and the longer we wait the more difficult will be the transition toward smaller, less intrusive government at all levels.
- We should have proctors to intervene as necessary when the situation warrants it using intelligent responses as opposed to using 'shoot first ask questions later' police blindly enforcing prearranged objectives.
- People will make mistakes requiring official intervention but this response should be applied in a surgical fashion, not with

a sledge hammer.
- People who are abusive towards other people or animals should be confronted and disciplined appropriately. All citizens have a responsibility to get involved to put a stop to this type of undesirable behavior.
- We *must* recognize and respect all other life forms on this planet and help them survive against the predations of man.
- We *must* stop despoiling the oceans with our refuse before it is too late to reverse the extinction of marine life that is surely coming.
- We have an obligation to leave the environment cleaner than we found it and this requires a proactive approach for successful results.
- We have an incredible opportunity that should not be wasted. We should focus a large part of our attention on developing the life sciences in an effort to populate as many other planetary objects as possible while at the same time cleaning and preserving our current home.
- Disabled individuals deserve every consideration without unwarranted skepticism.
- People deserve to live and die with dignity, as they choose, when they choose.
- The state is responsible for maintaining essential public services such that each person has access to clean water, clean air and pesticide-free foodstuffs, and on the flip side, the disposal of processed materials.
- The state is responsible for providing for the national defense. Each qualified individual must serve two years assisting in this effort.
- Any show of force will be met in kind.

- Change is inevitable; we can go with the flow or resist the tide knowing that each alternative has its own set of consequences, not always good, not always bad.
- The human mind should be free to explore whatever undiscovered vistas await.
- The blood of true patriots built this country and only the blood of true patriots can keep the dream alive.

Chapter 15

FROM HERE TO WHEREVER

When the power of The People is concentrated into the hands of The Few, in this case The 545, Predictable Things Happen.

The Few have made it their mandate to decide for Everyone Else what can be done, when it can be done, where it can be done, how it can be done, why it can be done and who is going to do it.

William Howard Taft, our 27th president, put it best when he stated that:

"No tendency is quite so strong in human nature as the desire to lay down rules of conduct for other people."

Recording and transmitting all of these various instructions in a lingo everyone can understand has not been an unqualified success story.

Just one federal agency has an operating manual containing in excess of four million words. Difficult words, legal sounding words, all put together in such a way as to make them all but illegible to the average Jane or Joe. Such agencies as this number in the hundreds at the very least. To say nothing at all of the other governmental bureaus, commissions, departments and offices, which number is surely in the thousands, each with their own set of rules to be followed or dispensed.

Should you inquire of the hypothetical man on the street regarding his familiarity with the multitude of laws he is subject to at that very moment he would most likely be able to tell you little beyond the usual and familiar six dozen things everyone needs to know in order to function in our society; say, for example, to avoid parking in front of a fire hydrant or to quickly push 'Door Close' when you see someone approaching your elevator.

Yes, we can unquestionably continue weaving an ever tighter legal stranglehold over and around the lives and activities of each and every individual. We have shown an absolute propensity for this very activity.

We can implement so many acts, bylaws, canons, charters, codes, covenants, laws, mandates, measures, ordinances, regulations, requirements, rules and statutes that you won't be able to turn around without bumping into one. In some ways this already is our present reality.

But is this truly a good idea?

Why do you think the founders of our country refused to do just this very thing?

```
"I would rather be exposed to the
inconveniencies attending too much liberty than
to those attending too small a degree of it."
— Thomas Jefferson (1743 - 1826)
— To Archibald Stuart on 23 December 1791
```

Yes, it is true, our forefathers, with the help of our foremothers, conceived a system to be used for the purpose of creating a set of laws any successful society needs in order to remain peaceful and cohesive while simultaneously promoting a business-friendly capitalist environment and the cause of scientific advancement.

The founders of our country did not attempt to describe or proscribe each and every circumstance that might ever occur but instead chose to enact general guidelines with some specific provisions to clarify the intended purpose of each law. More importantly, they left the door open for future generations to modify or expand this set of laws as changing circumstances dictated.

We definitely do need some laws for the common good, for public safety, sanitary systems and such, and I believe everyone recognizes this necessity. No question about this.

```
"The more corrupt the state, the more numerous
the laws."
   —Tacitus (AD56 - 117), Roman Historian
```

What we do not need are an excessive number of over-complicated laws that only one highly trained, specialized group of people have any real chance of deciphering and subsequently must therefore act as the only source of alleged intelligent interpretation for the rest of us. Sadly, the people who create these laws are the very same people we must trust to explain them to us in a language we can understand. You may be deluding yourself if you believe nothing is ever lost during translation.

Correct me if I am wrong but there may be a built-in conflict here between the people who make the rules and who generally exempt themselves from same, and the people actually affected by these rules: those who must live with this yoke around their necks.

```
"You delight in laying down laws,
Yet you delight more in breaking them.
Like children playing by the ocean who build
```

sand-towers with constancy and then destroy them with laughter."

— Kahlil Gibran (1883 – 1931), Artist, Poet & Writer

— From *The Prophet*

This original system of governance, which started out with such grandiose tenets, has long been sorely abused and willfully misused by those with enough money and influence to sway the vote however desired, thus permitting passage of legislation single-mindedly favorable to their own cause or efforts with complete disregard for the consequences to the society at large.

This does not make the system a bad thing. It does make *abuse* of the system a bad thing.

You don't have to believe me. Simply read your history books.

Need specific examples? OK, here are a few, in no particular order:

<u>Prohibition</u> of things people consume.

Alcoholic beverages:

Many places, most notable failures include:

  1901 to 1948 in Canada.

  1914 to 1925 in Russia and the Soviet Union.

  1920 to 1933 in the United States.

Drugs:

Well, this is a biggee. Been going on for a very long time in one form or another.

Ramped up in earnest in the early 20th century. In some places you forfeit your life for this 'offense'. In some places you forfeit your life even if you are not involved. This is happening *now*, today. Granted, we ordinarily have little or nothing to say about events occurring in other countries, but some folks do follow our lead now and again.

Prohibition serves only to spike both the interest in and the price of any given product thus making possible insane profits, which, in turn, drives people to perform insane acts they ordinarily would not even consider or that would not be necessary in the first place should the situation be reversed.

Governments worldwide, and particularly the United States, have invested **huge** sums to 'fight' this 'scourge'. And I do mean huge. Really huge. As in trillions of your taxpayer dollars huge.

Only problem is there is no scourge and never has been.

```
"When any government, or any church for that
matter, undertakes to say to its subjects, This
you may not read, this you must not see, this
you are forbidden to know, the end result is
tyranny and oppression no matter how holy the
motives."
  — Robert A. Heinlein (1907 – 1988), Writer
```

We can pretty much eliminate this entire 'problem' simply by eliminating the demand. This is easily accomplished by making all substances readily available, for a price, naturally, to consenting adults. Much of this process remains to be worked out but we already know that black markets disappear when legitimate channels of distribution are established.

I think We The People have provided enough support to black markets worldwide and it is time to put a stop to this nonsense. Too many people are being hurt by all these (unnecessary) under-the-table shenanigans.

We can easily establish places where people can go to indulge their desires under semi-controlled circumstances, say a large parkland complex with small cabins affording privacy and convenience at a reasonable price, where you can enter any time you like but you can exit only when medically declared clean enough to do so.

Who needs 'illegal' (and potentially dirty) very expensive substances when you can have anything you want, guaranteed medical grade and clean, just around the bend for only a moderate expenditure?

```
"It has been my experience that folks who
have no vices have very few virtues."
— Abraham Lincoln (1809 - 1865), 16th U.S.
President
```

The demand may initially spike simply out of the sheer novelty effect but "fer shure" will drop off eventually, probably much quicker than many expect, because most people actually have no use for this stuff.

There will of course always be some who will want to try mind altering substances. Let's give them a place to do so. And with no stigma attached. Why not? It can't possibly be worse than what we are doing now because what we are doing now is far, far worse, by any description. By orders of magnitude. And far more damaging to our society.

For the record, marijuana is *not* a mind altering substance. Usage of this substance does not cause one to lose touch with reality, it does not produce hallucinations or any other such symptoms, nor does it cause anyone to go loco. This misinformation has been widely advertised, however.

Insufferable Indifference - The Mocking of America

Eliminate the novelty, the profit and the *mystique* involved with drug usage and the vast majority of people will simply lose interest.

The Vietnam War. (1959-1975) Huge mistake. The only big winner here was the military / industrial complex supporting these efforts.

The Iraq War. Attacked on 20 March 2003 using false claims to inflame sentiment against the then current, now hanged, ruler, who had been in charge since 1979. And again, the only apparent winners here are those companies having contracts with the U.S. government to supply the goods and services necessary to wage this conflict.

The Patriot Act. (2001) Another huge mistake. There is no obvious winner here, but there is clearly a whole country full of losers.

The fruits of liberty can be easily spoiled using mediocrity and unswerving conformance to doctrine. The act of complete complacency, often manifested by The People, or so it seems, by ignoring their power as a group, spells d-i-s-a-s-t-e-r for the rights of the individual.

The question is, are we doomed to continue in the present mode? Or dare I say: we are doomed if we continue in the present mode.

Can we not change course and try something boldly new and innovative without destroying our ethics and our oh so comfortable society?

I accept the fact that my accumulated knowledge, while it may seem like a lot to me, is in reality only a miniscule fraction of the actual amount of all the knowledge obtainable in this universe.

```
"Anyone who isn't confused doesn't really
understand the situation."
     - Edward R. Murrow (1908 - 1965), Journalist
```

I know enough, however, to realize that this country, my country, faces serious challenges which the "business as usual" attitude cannot begin to cope with, and to say that I am concerned about the outcome we all face would be putting it mildly.

I do not have all the answers since I don't as yet have all the questions, and even if I did have all the questions I still would not have all the answers. I'm certainly not going to try to influence your thinking one way or another because I learned about information falling on deaf ears the hard way.

I believe it was Mr. Louis L'Amour (1908 - 1988) who popularized this expression: "you have to fork your own broncs". The extension to this is, of course, fork or be forked.

```
"You can avoid reality, but you cannot avoid
the consequences of avoiding reality."
  — Ayn Rand (1905 - 1982), Writer, Philosopher
```

The Few reward themselves and their supporters with an ever increasing orgy of expenditures even as they work diligently to identify legal means of stripping Everyone Else of all possessions.

We must find a way to eliminate the profit motive for any elected representative.

Getting elected to any position of office is called a term of service because these people are supposed to *serve*, not be served. Holding public office is supposed to be a sacrifice; you must set aside your own personal business pursuits, at least temporarily, in favor of working for the benefit of all.

Instead, The People have allowed 'our servants' to create and sustain a lavish lifestyle of privilege and luxury well beyond what the common man or woman can ever hope to achieve, and in many cases well beyond what the elected individual had before they were elected. They have also awarded themselves lifetime pensions 'for service rendered'. We The People need to reverse these automatic rewards which the undeserving have endowed themselves with.

The practice of accepting campaign contributions whether declared or otherwise in lieu of expected favoritism and cronyism once elected must be ended. This one activity is at the root of all boondoggles gratuitously dispensed by *elected* government officials in the past, the present, and in the future if we don't put a stop to it.

We must find a way to select individuals for public service based on their actual *qualifications* to serve instead of their personality traits or their outward appearance or their speaking or acting abilities. Electing unqualified individuals to office is a big part of our problem.

The overall size of government should be reduced to a minimum sustainable organization embracing intelligence, research and planning rather than reactionary pomposity as the tool of choice to be used when enacting (or de-enacting) laws.

We need to make sure the folks who make the laws are every bit as subject to them as everyone else is. No exceptions. And no special privileges.

Ultimately, those who are unwilling to carry the torch of liberty condemn themselves to watching it be extinguished on the altar of platitude.

```
"America will never be destroyed from the
outside. If we falter, and lose our freedoms,
it will be because we destroyed ourselves."
 — Abraham Lincoln (1809 - 1865), 16th U.S.
President
```

It seems to me that we need to focus on what is really important. Survival as a species is really important!

Employing large groups of people whose sole purpose in life is to minutely monitor the daily activities of The People and what they choose to ingest, this activity is not important, aside from the enforcement of standard safety protocols. People should be free to make their own life choices without undo interference. People should be free to make their own mistakes unfettered by authority.

Creating more victimless crimes and selectively applying same by using large armies of enforcers; building more and more courts and prisons to 'process' 'offenders', this is not where our attention should be directed.

Such thinking is inherently wrong and serves only to distract us away from the things we *should* be thinking about. All that actually gets accomplished by following this established policy is that hordes of people are kept busy doing things they need not be doing. It goes without saying that they could instead be doing something else far more productive in nature. Something more in tune with our actual needs as a race on the brink of experiencing natural disasters the likes of which will shake the very foundations of our society right to the core.

Instead of all this inward-focused personal micromanagement, *why not* turn our vision outward, even if only for a moment, and try to explore the possibilities? What do we stand to lose? Time? We have this in abundance. *Why not* use a little time in an attempt to consider a more positive outcome for the rights of the individual in the future? Survival, for example, this sounds fairly positive.

Perhaps we each should each make a list of what we consider to be important, then compare notes and act on our findings! *Why not?* We will achieve more tangible results by working together.

Tops on my list is developing a program supporting the survival and export of ALL life on this rock we call home. This one item alone can keep all of us very busy for a very long time.

Like liberty, life cannot be restored once lost. Extinction is forever. Look it up!

We must begin behaving properly, and soon, to take full advantage of this one magical opportunity we have been given to colonize the stars or it is the human race that will become extinct.

We will not be missed. No one will ever know we were here. And rightly so.

Nature does not reward stupidity even if dumb luck does occasionally prevail.